THE
POEMS
OF
SAINT
JOHN
OF THE
CROSS

BOOKS BY WILLIS BARNSTONE

POETRY

Poems of Exchange
Notes for a Bible
From This White Island
Antijournal
A Day in the Country
New Faces of China
China Poems

TRANSLATIONS

Sappho
Greek Lyric Poetry
Physiologus Theobaldi Episcopi (Bishop Theobald's Bestiary)
The Song of Songs
The Poems of Saint John of the Cross
Eighty Poems of Antonio Machado
The Poems of Mao Tse-tung (with Ko Ching-Po)

ANTHOLOGIES

Modern European Poetry
Spanish Poetry: From its Beginnings through the
    Nineteenth Century
Concrete Poetry: A World View (with Mary Ellen Solt)
Eighteen Texts: Writings by Contemporary Greek Authors
Major Women Poets (with Aliki Barnstone)

EDITIONS

New Spoon River by Edgar Lee Masters
Rinconte y Cortadillo by Miguel de Cervantes
    (with Hugh Harter)
The Solitudes by Luis de Gongora
Mexico before Cortez: Art, History, and Legend
    by Ignacio Bernal

THE POEMS OF SAINT JOHN OF THE CROSS

English Versions and Introduction by Willis Barnstone

A NEW DIRECTIONS BOOK

*For their many helpful suggestions, my thanks to José Donoso,
Ruth Stone, Robert and Brenda Schildgen, and Norma Grasso.*

Published by arrangement with Indiana University Press,
Bloomington, Indiana, which publishes a clothbound
edition of this book.

First published as New Directions Paperbook 341 in 1972
Manufactured in the United States of America
Published simultaneously in Canada by
George J. McLeod Ltd., Toronto

New Directions Books are published for James Laughlin
by New Directions Publishing Corporation,
80 Eighth Avenue, New York 10011

SIXTH PRINTING

FOR
MIGUEL
ENGUÍDANOS

CONTENTS

CONTENTS

San Juan de la Cruz was a poet of paradox. He wrote few poems, or if he wrote more than we have, made little effort to preserve them.[1] Yet in the eleven central poems of his work, we have a poet unsurpassed in the Spanish language, a companion in quality to Sappho and Li Po, to Emily Dickinson and Cavafy. He was widely eclectic and openly derivative, yet among the most original poets in any tongue. He was not at all concerned with his place as a poet or the worth of poetry in itself, yet poetry was so important to him that it was, he wrote in his commentaries, the only means of expressing the ineffable.

In San Juan we feel the deepest, most withdrawn sense of solitude, though his theme was union. He sought freedom from the senses although his own poems comprise the most intensely erotic literature written in the Iberian peninsula from the time of the Moors to García Lorca. Although he was a monk who had taken vows of chastity, his allegory to express oneness with an absolute being was the sexual climax of lovers. Usually he wrote in the first person singular, but his poems are never autobiographical in the ordinary sense of small incidents, as in poems of Quevedo or Lope; he always wore a mask—normally that of the female lover—yet behind the mask the lyrical speaker of the poems is universally personal and, in an almost spatial sense, profoundly within San Juan himself. He looked for darkness to find fire, and was comforted by his unknowing, which gave him hope of knowing. He withdrew from the world to be closer to his God, yet nature and human love are the key to his poetry. To rise, San Juan fell to the blackest bottomland. To live, he had to die in life, his poems say. To waken he closed his eyes in order to see in the black night. As in the Platonic allegory of the cave, each step toward the sun of fire produced instant blindness and the sun itself oblivion. And while he moved toward the invisible, he gave us the things of this world in startling light. What he saw, he tells us, left him stunned and stammering, yet his words, far from being sloppy and vague, are clear in sound and meaning, with the plain economy of a perfect circle.

San Juan was persecuted during his lifetime, tortured and crippled by his accusers. Yet he is said to have been a man of unshakable equanimity, without rancor. Unlike those of Fray Luis, his poems were of joy rather than resentment, and when severe, only against himself. They never shout, are never wild or inflated; they are precise, and express beauty and intense passion with simple ease. San Juan had two hours: the dark night of *Noche oscura* and *La fonte,* and the pristine day of *Cántico espiritual;* in both moments he was a poet of love and ecstasy. No poet in the West has traveled so thoroughly in the bright and black air of ecstasy.

HIS LIFE

The poet's family name was Juan de Yepes. The name is brief and curiously, in a Spanish class sense, *humilde* (humble) –far different from the resonant quality of San Juan de la Cruz, which, as Jorge Guillén points out, even translates into other languages "with outstanding success: Saint Jean de la Croix, San Giovanni della Croce, Saint John of the Cross." [2] Juan de Yepes' childhood was correspondingly *humilde.* Born in 1542 in Fontiveros, a village in the heartland of Castile, between Avila and Salamanca, he was the son of an impoverished weaver.

Like Fray Luis and Santa Teresa, the other major Spanish mystics, he came in part from a family of *conversos*–"new Christians" who had been forced to convert from Judaism. A few years after his birth his father died, leaving a widow and three sons in deeper poverty. Juan worked variously as a painter, carpenter, and tailor. His mother worked at the family loom.

In his adolescence the family moved to Medina del Campo, a larger, somewhat prosperous town nearby, where Juan worked at one time begging alms in the streets for a hospital that treated syphilitic patients. Most of his day he spent in the streets or at the hospital, but he was allowed time off to receive his first real education at a newly founded Jesuit school. He was evidently an exceptionally good student, learned Latin well, and remained at the school until he was twenty-one. Then he was offered the chaplaincy of the hospital at which he had been working, but chose instead to take vows as a Carmelite friar. He took the name of Juan de Santo Matías.

The next year, 1564, he went to the University of Salamanca, where he remained for four years. At that time Salamanca, along with Bologna, Paris, and Oxford, was one of the great university centers in Europe. We know little of his life there, but some intriguing questions arise. Did he know or study with Fray Luis de León, the great humanist and mystical poet? In 1572 Fray Luis was to be imprisoned in a dungeon in Valladolid for, among other things, having translated the Song of Songs directly from the original Hebrew of the Old Testament. The Song of Songs, or Canticles, was to become the source of San Juan's most ambitious poem, *Cántico espiritual*. We do know, however, that in 1567 Juan de Santo Matías met Teresa de Jesús, a woman already in her fifties, who was then beginning her mission to reform the Carmelite order. It was a decisive meeting in his life.

Teresa's reform was in part a turning away from affluence, in part a return to prayer and contemplation, to austerity and the road toward mystical union. She was founding small convents and monasteries throughout Spain, and also arousing intense enmity among the unreformed Carmelites. She asked the young friar for his help. He took vows in 1568, changing his name to Juan de la Cruz.

His first assignment was a small poor farmhouse, converted into a hermitage, which he shared with a few monks at Duruelo, only a few miles from Fontiveros, Juan's birthplace. Next we hear of Juan de la Cruz as master of novices at Pastrana, near Alcalá de Henares, and then as a teacher in a Carmelite college in Alcalá itself. In 1572 Teresa brought him to the unreformed Carmelite convent of Encarnación at Avila. Teresa had been sent by her enemies to this unreformed convent, where she had formerly spent twenty years. But in the course of her time there, between her influence and that of Juan de la Cruz, the nuns' confessor and spiritual director, the majority of the nuns were won over to the reform movement. An election among the nuns was held to determine the new prioress, and Teresa, who a few years before had been the prioress, was certain to be elected to this position. The Provincial of the Carmelite Order came to supervise the election and threatened excommunication to those who supported Teresa. In her letters Teresa describes how the vote was then taken; the defiant nuns elected Teresa, whereupon the Provincial intervened, excommunicating and cursing the nuns who had voted for the reform candidate, burned their ballots, declared the election void, and appointed his own candidate. The sequel to the election was on the night of December 2 or 3, 1577, when a gang broke into the house where Fray Juan de la Cruz was living and carried him off to a dark prison in the Carmelite Priory in Toledo.[3] Fray Juan was Teresa's spiritual accomplice, and the Carmelite authorities in Spain wanted, at any price, to stop the spread of the reform movement.

Immediately after his arrest, Teresa wrote to Philip II saying that she preferred to see him in the hands of the Moors rather than in those of the Mitigated Carmelites.

The Moors would at least have more pity, she wrote. Juan de la Cruz's unlit cell was actually a small cupboard, not high enough for him to stand erect. He was taken each day to the refectory, where he was given bread, water, and sardine scraps on the floor. Then he was subjected to the circular discipline: while he knelt on the ground, the monks walked around him, scouring his bare back with their leather whips. At first a daily occurrence, this was later restricted to Fridays, but he was tortured with such zeal that his shoulders remained crippled for the rest of his life.

San Juan suffered other torments too. For most of six months he was given no change of clothing and was infested with lice. He had dysentery from the food and thought he was being poisoned. The windowless, airless cell was unheated in the winter, stifling hot in the summer months. We are told that amid all this one night he heard a *villancico*–a type of popular song–being sung in the street:

> Muérome de amores,
> carillo, ¿qué haré?
> —¡Que te mueras, alahé!
>
> I am dying of love,
> darling, what shall I do?
> Just die then, alahé!

It is difficult to explain to one who cannot read Spanish the poignant charm of these lines. They have the salt and ease of popular Spanish poetry, the pathos and paradox found in San Juan. Apparently San Juan was carried away into ecstasy by the beauty and thought of the lyrics. He was given paper and pen by a new jailer who had been kind to him, and during this time he wrote from seventeen to thirty stanzas of *Cántico espiritual* and completed *La fonte* and probably *Noche oscura*. *La fonte*, with its refrain *aunque es de noche* (although it is night) speaks of his faith amid darkness. The poem *Noche oscura (Black Night)* is a love poem, an allegory of mystical union, and in an immediate sense an escape through the dark night.

In August of 1578 he resolved to escape. Gerald Brenan, in his interesting study which appeared in *Horizon*, May 1947, recounts:

> On the eve of the Assumption of the Virgin the Prior of the Convent entered his cell, and after kicking him brutally and rating him for his disobedience, promised to release him if he would abandon the Reform and return to the mitigated rule. Juan replied that he could not break his vows, but asked if he might be allowed to say mass on the following day, as it was the feast of the Virgin. The Prior angrily refused and went out. But that night Our Lady appeared to Juan in a dream. Filling his cell with light, she commanded him to escape, promising her assistance. This dream drew out an early memory. Once as a little boy at Fontiveros he had fallen into a pond. As he struggled in the mud and water he had seen a well-dressed lady on the bank whom he had taken to be the Virgin. He had stretched out his arms to her, but with closed fists because his hands were too dirty to take hers. Then someone else had pulled him out. He now felt assured that, in spite of his weakness, with her help he would be able to escape from prison.[4]

A few days after this incident San Juan prepared his venture. After prying loose the hinges of his cell door, shortly past two in the morning he stepped over the bodies of some sleeping friars and lowered himself down from a balcony to the city wall by means of a rope made from strips of his blankets and own clothing. From the wall he jumped into a courtyard, enclosed by high walls, which somehow–he said with the Virgin's help–he managed to scale. He found himself free in the streets of Toledo.

San Juan took refuge in a convent of the Discalced Carmelites. On this first day of his escape, while still recovering from immediate hardships, he dictated part of his poetry which he had not been able to write in his cell. It was too dangerous, however, for him to remain in Toledo and he was first taken to his home and then sent to a small hermitage in Andalusia, El Calvario, by the upper waters of the Guadalquivir.

San Juan spent six months in El Calvario, among the happiest in his life. Referring to his imprisonment, he wrote in a letter: "After the whale swallowed me up and vomited me out. . . ." [5] From the darkness of the whale he came into the clarity and beauty of the Andalusian landscape. Here in solitude his career as a poet was fixed. As far as we know, during this grand period he completed the corpus of his poetry, except for the last stanzas of *Cántico espiritual,* which he finished in Baeza and revised later in Granada, and *¡Oh Llama de amor viva!,* also written in Granada. He was then thirty-seven. After this he was a teacher, founder, and officer of reformed Carmelites and, according to the verdict of the later Church, a saint. He also wrote his voluminous commentaries on the poems–his anti-poems one might call them. But he wrote little or no more poetry; at least he wrote few poems he wished or attempted to preserve. As in the case of Rimbaud, however, about whom we now have evidence to date poems years after *Saison en Enfer,* which had been thought his last burst of fire in an equally brief career, it is fair to speculate that San Juan must also have continued, at least sporadically, to give expression in poetry to a life which continued to be characterized by meditation and rapture *(arrobamiento)* .

Following this brief period of recovery and poetry at El Calvario, San Juan was sent, in 1579, to Baeza to direct a newly formed Carmelite college. These were less happy years. In his letters he records that here in the city among the Andalusians–as opposed to his desert retreat–he felt exiled. He consoled himself by making frequent trips to nearby Beas de Segura, a convent of Castilian nuns founded a few years before by Teresa. The parallel here between San Juan and Antonio Machado, Spain's other major poet of contemplation and landscape, is striking.

In somewhat desperate letters to Miguel de Unamuno, Machado writes how as a teacher in Baeza he felt lost and exiled, how he consoled himself by frequent solitary and meditative walks on the road to nearby Ubeda—where San Juan was to die. In both solitary poets the act of contemplation is central in their lives and art. In San Juan the most persistent tradition speaks of him at El Calvario, in Baeza, later in Granada and Segovia, sitting for hours alone, in the fields under some trees or in a convent tower or in some secluded cell, contemplating the spectacle of nature both during the day and for hours at night.

From Baeza, San Juan was sent in 1582 to Granada, where he was Prior of a new house, El Convento de los Mártires. This monastery was on the hill of the Alhambra, which looks out at the white Sierra Nevada across one of the most extraordinary views in Spain. San Juan speaks of the beauty of the land in his commentaries. Then after 1585 his life became much more turbulent and demanding. He became Vicar Provincial for Andalusia and had to journey all over the south of Spain, usually on a donkey. In 1588 he was made Prior in Segovia; there he gave himself to meditation, and, according to his biographers, his spiritual life reached its summit. By his own testimony he experienced mystical union both in Granada and in Segovia.

Meanwhile the Carmelite reformers had triumphed, at least insofar as they were recognized by the Pope as a separate organization with their own Provincial. But with the election of Nicolás Doria as the Provincial, replacing Teresa's and San Juan's protector Gracián, the trouble of internal disorder came. Teresa had died in 1582. Ana de Jesús, her successor and a close friend to Juan, was imprisoned. Other followers of Teresa and San Juan were exiled to remote convents. San Juan attempted to intervene in Ana de Jesús' convent in Madrid to support the rights of the nuns to use the secret ballot and govern themselves democratically (in accordance with a recent brief from the Pope). The issue of the liberty to vote was the same as that at Avila which had led to his imprisonment at Toledo. Now he was stripped of all office and exiled to La Peñuela, a desert house in Andalusia. Evidence was collected against him, some of it tragi-comic, such as a false accusation by a nun in Málaga that she had been kissed by Fray Juan through the grille of her window. At Beas de Segura, his favorite convent, the nuns destroyed all papers and letters from him, for fear of being implicated with the heretic monk. There was a move to expel him from the order, and only his sickness spared him this last step. Suffering from fever and ulcers on the legs, he went to nearby Ubeda for treatment. But the Prior refused to give him the barest necessities and treated him with vengeful hostility, coming each day to his cell to insult him. The ulcers spread. His body was literally rotting away. He died at midnight on December 14, 1591.

Juan's death set the town of Ubeda in a mood of panic. He was held to be a saint, and though it was cold and raining, crowds entered the convent that night to tear off part of his clothing, bandages, and even ulcerous flesh. He was buried in Ubeda. Segovia wanted his corpse, however, and finally after nine months a royal warrant was obtained and he was dug up at night. According to the accepted legend, he had not decayed and gave off a sweet aroma. When he was canonized in 1726, this was held as one of the proofs of his saintliness. Such was the desire to possess something of the saint—in life he had been simply a friar, a poet, and a mystic—that he was deprived of a leg, which he left behind at Ubeda, an arm in Madrid, and fingers in various holy places. After he reached Segovia, a counterappeal was made to Rome and his remaining limbs were cut off and sent back to Ubeda. San Juan suffered the felicity of mystical dying, the harsh pain of bodily death, and finally a macabre disfigurement as his eager admirers fought over his remains. It was the ultimate paradox of a man whose life was marked by torture and rapture, a man who always sought the harsh night, the small cell, the lonely exile, yet saw through the

night, was entranced by beauty, and gave himself entirely
to his quest for love and light.

The art and victory of San Juan's poetry is unique: with
only a few poems he achieves great variety, each poem a
distinct world, revealing a new possibility of expression.
In Spanish literature particularly, where the prolific, or
overprolific, writer is the norm–Lope, Cervantes, Galdós
–San Juan's few poems bring him to the highest peaks
of literature. He is comparable to those Greek poets–
Archilochos, Sappho, Bakchylides–whose work has come
down to us only as scattered fragments, yet who neverthe-
less are fully defined poetic personalities and whose lyric
voice, especially today, speaks to us with equal or greater
force than a more fully preserved Horace or Virgil.

Formally, San Juan's poetry derives from three poetic
traditions: the Italian, the Spanish and Portuguese, and
the Hebrew. In his study *La poesía de San Juan de la
Cruz*, Dámaso Alonso traces in detail the origin of many
of San Juan's lines from these sources. The Italian in-
fluence in San Juan came to him through Garcilaso de
la Vega (1500–1539), who, with Boscán, was the first
known poet to write Castilian poetry in a variety of
Italian forms. The *lira,* which San Juan uses in his
three central poems *Noche oscura, Cántico espiritual,*
and *¡Oh Llama de amor viva!,* first appeared in Spanish
in Garcilaso's poem *A la flor de Gnido*. But Dámaso
Alonso convincingly demonstrates that while San Juan
knew the work of Garcilaso, his immediate source was an
intermediary, Sebastián de Córdoba. In 1575 Sebastián
de Córdoba published a volume entitled *Obras de Boscán
y Garcilaso trasladadas a materias cristianas y religiosas
(Works of Boscán and Garcilaso Transformed into Chris-
tian and Religious Materials)*. In a mediocre way
Garcilaso's and Boscán's poems are recast *a lo divino.*
Alonso suggests that San Juan took the symbolization of
the fountain (faith) in *La fonte* and the symbol of the

tree in *El pastorcico* from Sebastián de Córdoba, as well as the central idea of *¡Oh Llama de amor viva!* from a stanza beginning *El fuego de amor vivo*. But directly from Garcilaso's *Egloga segunda* we find elements of both *Noche oscura* and *¡Oh Llama de amor viva!* in

> La quinta noche, en fin, mi cruda suerte
> queriéndome llevar do *se rompiese*
> *aquesta tela de la vida fuerte,*
> hizo de mi choza *me saliese*
> *por el silencio de la noche oscura.* . . .
> (lines 5333–37, italics mine)

In addition we find a general pastoral vocabulary which San Juan borrows equally from Garcilaso and the Bible.

A word of caution, however, about the poet's use of a Garcilaso recast and made acceptably pious and banal. While Sebastián de Córdoba took a pastoral work, in the Greco-Roman and Petrarchan tradition, changed its diction and gave it an abstract message, squeezing Christian theology out of pastoral love, San Juan never proceeds from particular to general. Rather, if we may assume that some of the concepts expressed in his commentaries were with him when he composed his lyrics, such conceptual abstractions disappeared in the course of composing the poem, for San Juan moves from general to particular images, and usually very sensual images which the reader, if he wants to, either by his own intuition or through the aid of the commentaries, may reinterpret conceptually *a lo divino*. Again another high paradox in San Juan: our poet receives the impact of a Garcilaso *a lo divino,* which in turn leads him to a highly concrete symbolization. Indeed, San Juan's symbols are so immediate and real in terms of human love and perception of nature that both Garcilaso and Sebastián de Córdoba seem nebulously distant from reality by comparison with the fire of San Juan's here and now.

The Spanish and Portuguese source in San Juan is evident in several ways. The most obvious *popular* or

Castilian quality of the poems is in the use of the *romance* (ballad) meters and *estribillos* (refrains). Like Lope, Gil Vicente, and Shakespeare, San Juan took popular poems, changed them and made them his own. He also wrote *glosas*; that is, he took the first stanza of an existent poem and wrote a commentary in verse. Thus we have in another poet, Pedro de Padilla:

> Por sola la hermosura
> nunca yo me perderé,
> sino por un no sé que,
> que se halla por ventura.

And in San Juan:

> Por toda la hermosura
> nunca yo me perderé,
> sino por un no sé que
> que se alcanza por ventura.[6]

In taking this simple love poem San Juan seizes upon the phrase *no sé qué*–similar to his *un no sé qué que quedan balbuciendo* (from *Cántico*) and *que me quedé balbuciendo* (from *Entréme donde no supe*)–which the poet uses onomatopoetically to show the stuttering state of the lover in ecstasy when he attempts to express the ineffable. He converts a love song into a lyric with a mystical reference. We see the same method used when he and Santa Teresa each write versions of

> Vivo sin vivir en mí,
> y de tan alta vida espero
> que muero porque no muero.

The theme of dying for love, dying because one does not die, living without life because one does not die, etc., is found in innumerable earlier Spanish poems, in both the courtly and the popular traditions. San Juan and Santa Teresa give the refrain *muero porque no muero* a distinctly metaphysical meaning in that the death in life they seek is not only that of human agony (the first *muero* in the phrase) but a temporary death within life (the second *muero*), a suspension of the senses and a departure from oneself, from man-perceived time and space, in order for the soul of man to unite with God.[7]

San Juan also relies on Spanish song for many of his images. The symbolism of the male falcon erotically pursuing the female heron is a commonplace in medieval literature, found in the bestiaries, in troubadour lyrics, and in folklore. In Spanish we find the symbolism of the hunt for love in popular *villancicos,* in the *cancionero anónimo,* in Gil Vicente and Juan del Encina. In San Juan's

> Tras de un amoroso lance,
> volé tan alto, tan alto,
> que le di a la caza alcance

the poet again takes a love lyric and makes it *a lo divino,* without losing any of its force on the immediate denotive level of its symbols.

A last example of Spanish-Portuguese tradition may be seen in *La fonte,* in such lines as

> Sé que no puede ser cosa tan bella,
> y que ninguno puede vadealla,
>   aunque es de noche.
> Bien sé que suelo en ella no se halla,
> y que ninguno puede vadealla,
>   aunque es de noche.

The parallelistic structure of the entire poem—the repetition of the *estribillo* and certain key phrases, such as *sé que*—is characteristic of the Portuguese and Galician *cosante.* It is also a central prosodic device in Hebrew poetry of the Old Testament, as in Job and the Song of Songs. In fact we see the same device of parallelism used in the *jarchas,* poems written in Spanish by Andalusians in Moslem Spain as early as the tenth century, which later appears in the Portuguese and Galician popular tradition.

The third major influence on the poetry of San Juan is the Hebrew poetry found in the Old Testament. San Juan's access to Biblical poetry was through the Vulgate–unlike Fray Luis, who translated directly from the Hebrew. Old Testament pastoral imagery appears throughout the poet's work, in his poems, prose, and also in the letters. But it must also be remembered that these pastoral elements–images like *ninfas de Judea*–are a blending of elements from Garcilaso and the Bible. In Garcilaso himself, we should note, the complex pastoral mode contains several sources, the European line of Theokritos, Virgil, and Petrarch, as well as the pastoral poetry of the Old Testament.

We find Biblical diction in many poems, in *El pastorcico* and *Noche oscura*: "y el ventalle de cedros aire daba" and "entre las azucenas olvidado." But the most striking example is in the *Cántico espiritual,* an imitation and interpretation in Spanish of the Song of Songs (the Canticles of King Solomon). The Song of Songs is a fragmentary collection of songs in dialogue form, which have enough coherence to be called a wedding idyll or ceremonial drama, yet enough lacunae and diversity to suggest that its origin may derive from folk song not only of Jewish but of neighboring cultures, including the Egyptian. In this paradoxical quality of overall esthetic coherence yet arbitrary sequence of events, indeed at times incoherence in the plot, the Biblical Song of Songs resembles San Juan's version. The unity of tone in *Cántico espiritual* is sustained so completely throughout that no stanza jars, whatever the order; there is change but no essential rupture in style and no diminution in the intensity of the beauty and passion expressed. And all this contributes to making the poem one of the few successful longer lyrics in literature. Yet in terms of logical sequence, it is one of the poorest examples of order. San Juan himself appears to have perceived this, and consequently wrote the poem in at least two versions, that of the codex of Sanlúcar de Barrameda and that of Jaén.[8]

In the second version San Juan corrects, or attempts to correct, the sequence in order to give it doctrinal order. It also contains an extra stanza. But the consensus of his most sympathetic critics is that the first version is superior. In any case, in both its first and second redactions, the poet has succeeded in reproducing a unified yet *fragmentary* song, and this is one of the most important, if curious, ways in which he has remained faithful to the Biblical text. He wrote the poem, he states in his prologue, "under the influence of abundant mystical intelligence [knowledge]"; we may assume that it was not a "mystical intelligence" of the author or authors of the Song of Songs which led to its present fragmentary state. But no matter. The artistic effect is the same. It may at this time be remembered, however, that early Christian writers could justify the inclusion of this collection of impassioned Jewish folk songs only as an allegory of the love of Christ for his Church: in San Juan the *esposo* (husband-Christ) and *esposa* (bride-Church-soul). For parallel reasons the Jews originally gave the speakers the names of King Solomon, The Shulamite, The Brothers, and The Chorus of the Daughters of Jerusalem in order to be able to keep the work within the holy canon.

From a very early period, then, this dramatic love poem was considered an allegory of divine love. San Juan used it in this way, but in giving his version an allegorical meaning he lost none of the original freshness.

Whole lines are incorporated from the Song of Songs into the *Cántico*.

> Do not despise me if
> you find the color of my flesh
> is brown. Look at me well,
> and then see how you
> endowed me with your grace and beauty.
>
> Catch us the little foxes,
> our vines already are in bloom;
> while we take a handful of
> the roses for our spray
> let no one in the hills appear.

INTRODUCTION

Stop, north wind of death
and come, south wind recalling love.
Breathe on my garden, let
aromas swell in the air,
my love will graze among the flowers.

One can observe even by comparing an English transla-
tion of the Bible with the above translation from Spanish
that every element in these three stanzas may be found in
the Song of Songs. San Juan takes lines here and there
from the Song of Songs and creates a new crazy-quilt
pattern–which he later alters in the second redaction–
from the original Biblical crazy-quilt. San Juan knew
perfectly well what he was doing. Words, order, reason,
knowledge are all inadequate to express the mystery of
love. He wrote in his prologue:

> And who can set in words that which He makes them
> to feel? And lastly who can express that which He
> makes them desire? Of a surety, none; nay, indeed,
> not the very souls through whom He passes. It is for
> this reason that, by means of figures, comparisons
> and similitudes, they allow something of that which
> they feel to overflow and utter secret mysteries from
> the abundance of the Spirit, rather than explain these
> things rationally.[9]

What is the nature of this mystery? What is the
mystical process and how relevant is it to the poems of
San Juan de la Cruz? First, it should be stated that in the
formal sense of the word, San Juan was a mystical poet–
but not because we may find, as in the poetry of Herbert,
Vaughan, Blake, Hopkins, and others, what some critics
call mystical tendencies or mystical implications. The
word "mystical" has been cheapened to mean anything
from mysterious, vaguely religious, to hermetic sym-
bolism and plain mystification. San Juan was a mystical
poet because in a formal sense his poems were written,
he himself states, as a result of *mystical knowledge,* and
in his commentaries he endeavors to explain the poems,

in great detail, *as steps toward the mystical union.* The question of whether mysticism is a valid religious experience or a form of hysteria, hallucination, psychedelic substitute, or sublimated sexual ecstasy, or even whether the poems themselves convey the mystical experience, is secondary and not the issue. The point I wish to make clear is that the appellation mystical poet–*Doctor Místico* as he was called–is correct in that San Juan was himself a mystic and the origin of his poems lies in the mystical experience. Perhaps in saying this we have said nothing, for what interests us after all is the poetry, not the poet, and to probe too deeply into the origin of a poem will probably plunge us into the genetic fallacy, where we confuse origin with achievement. Yet, unless we carefully distinguish between origin and achievement, our ultimate interpretation of the poems will also be confused and misleading.

The particular mystical tradition from which San Juan derives is complex and is surely one of the fields most poorly illuminated by scholarship. Few have the necessary languages, knowledge, and objectivity to deal with the subject, and as a result we have much that is willful and wishful, and very little else. Certain facts can be stated in a general way, however, about the background of Spanish mysticism and the nature of the experience itself.

In the Iberian peninsula the best-known mystics, as distinguished from such earlier German counterparts as à Kempis and Eckhart, were important *literary* as well as religious figures. We have Judah Halevi, 1085–1140, Ibn Arabi, 1165–1240, Raimundo Lull, 1233–1315, and San Juan's contemporaries Fray Luis de León and Santa Teresa. Raimundo Lull, known as the "Illuminated Doctor," is the author of a famous poem *Cántico del amigo y del amado,* which parallels San Juan's work in diction and thought. Lull was a missionary among the Moors of Spain and North Africa, to whom he preached in Arabic. His own verse and prose show the rich sensual imagery of Arabic poetry which we also find in San Juan.

Lull was one of the main ties between Islamic and Christian mysticism in the Iberian peninsula.

Another important source for Spain's mystical-literary authors was Jewish mysticism. A key intellectual document in the sixteenth century was León Hebreo's extraordinarily popular book *Dialoghi d'amore*, 1535, published first in Italian and then in Spanish. In his volume León Hebreo, a Spanish Jew exiled to Naples, proposes a philosophy of love as a means of obtaining union with God. The book is Neo-Platonic in nature, and reveals, in addition to Biblical language, the thoughts and lexicon of Ben Gabirol, Maimonides, and the *Cabala*. We have seen that the allegory of human love appears in many sources to which San Juan had access. None, however, with the exception of the Song of Songs, was more available to him, or more in the spiritual climate of Spain in the sixteenth century, than the words and message of León Hebreo.

With the strictness of orthodoxy following the Counter-Reformation, mysticism was an outlet for the spiritual energy of such heretics as San Juan, Santa Teresa, and Fray Luis (all of whom were to pay dearly for their individual spiritual roads and means of reaching ideas beyond the confines of Catholic theology). It should finally be mentioned that these Spanish mystics also derived from more general mystical currents than the forementioned Christian, Islamic, and Jewish manifestations found in Spain. From antiquity throughout the Renaissance the roots of mysticism were to be found in both West and East, from the early Christian saints and Neo-Platonism to Indian Brahmanism and Persian Sufism. The complexity of cross-currents between these major movements is staggering. But for our purposes it may be well first to remember Plato, the foremost figure of both a secular and a religious variety in early Western mysticism, the philosopher and poet from whom so many fundamental notions ultimately derive. Plato's basic separation of mind and matter, his concept of the immortality of the soul (*Phaedo*), of human love

(*Symposium*), of the various levels of cognition (the divided-line concept in *The Republic*) and the oneness of absolute truth, beauty, and the good which one may attain only through powers above the level of reason— all these are basic to the mystic. Plato also makes clear that a knowledge of absolutes can never be fully conveyed, even in dialogues. He uses the allegory of the cave as a useful method of suggesting the ineffable, but the stunning and blinding light of the sun's illumination, he claims, cannot be fully explained; to know it, it must be experienced. In San Juan, poetry brings us closer to the experience of that light than conceptual explanations.

We may now ask what steps San Juan followed in his mystical experience and how these steps appear in the poems. To summarize briefly, the soul may reach union with God when man goes through three basic stages: 1. *via purgativa*, 2. *via iluminativa*, 3. *via unitiva*. In the first, purgative, stage, through discipline and will one escapes from the dark night of the senses, annihilating the self; in the second stage, an illumination, one sees and feels the presence of God. In the third, man becomes one with God; man's soul (the *esposa*, or bride) is consumed in perfect love as it joins in spiritual matrimony with God (*esposo*, or husband). The steps are characterized by pain and darkness, by journeying by the great light of faith, by a rising into ecstasy, union, and oblivion. A fourth stage is sometimes added, which is the peace and beatitude that follow the union.

San Juan speaks of his journey as a negative way, a passive night of the soul, where through unknowing one comes upon a mystical understanding; his basic thought is not essentially distant from Keats' negative capability, Bergson's intuition and duration, or even the Socratic idea of knowing more because one knows nothing. All these notions have one common basis: to see, understand, and create, one must first erase previous notions, habits, and patterns of thinking, in order to achieve a *tabula rasa* or virginal state; from the nothing or *nada* or dark night, one is prepared freshly to see, understand, and create. There is no psychic mystery here. The act of creation, almost by definition, demands a rejection or transformation of what is old before a new creation. The diction associated with creation–revelation, intuition, inspiration–reinforces San Juan's notion of *algo* or *a no sé qué* from *nada*, "something" from "nothing," light from darkness. The irony and paradox of San Juan's notion of something from nothing appears again and again in his commentaries and poetry:

Sin arrimo y con arrimo,
sin luz y a oscuras viviendo,
todo me voy consumiendo.

Without a place and with a place
to rest–living darkly with no ray
of light–I burn my self away.

Especially in the minor poems [10] the process of mysticism is stated very clearly. One need have no fore-knowledge of Saint John or of his commentaries to perceive the mystical diction and concepts. The poem *Entréme donde no supe* (*I Came Into the Unknown*) or to give its codex title *Coplas del mismo hechas sobre un éxtasis de alta contemplación* (Verses by the same author about an ecstasy of high contemplation) describes the mystical act. It is a fine poem but it remains essentially a description of conditions necessary for the mystical experience, of characteristics of the mystical experience, and of the effects of that experience. It is not, however, the experience itself or an allegorical equivalent of it. Two minor poems, *Sin arrimo y con arrimo* and *Tras de un amoroso lance,* clearly do use a mystical vocabulary and come closer to expressing something of the experience. In the three central poems, however, we have an intense experience, but the nature of its presentation is totally different. San Juan informs us that the "experience overflows in figures and similes, and from the abundance of their spirit pour out secrets and mysteries rather than rational explanations."[11] The figures and similes–or allegory–of these three poems may suggest a mystical reference. But unlike the minor poems, the central poems use little or no diction which is conceptually mystical, and a well-informed reader may see nothing at all mystical in these three love poems, for even key phrases such as "dark night," "lover transformed in the lover," "forgotten among the lilies" may be read to mean exactly what they say: a love encounter between a woman and a man. Need we then, or should we, read the poems imposing on them our knowledge of their mystical origin or, as the commentaries prove, their mystical intention?

To answer this critical question, we should first state the relationship of the commentaries to the poems. On the one hand, the commentaries were written after the poems, depend on them, and are inextricably tied to them; without them the commentaries have no axis. On the other, the poems are autonomous, do not depend on the commentaries for their meaning, and, indeed, explanations are often distant, if not far-fetched. San Juan himself seems to have understood the relation of poem to commentary better than most of his critics and readers. He writes:

> Since these stanzas then were composed in a love flowing from abundant mystical understanding, I cannot explain them adequately, nor is it my intention to do so. I only wish to shed some general light on them, since your Reverence has desired this of me. I believe such an explanation will be more suitable. It is better to explain the utterances of love in their broadest sense so that each one may derive profit from them according to the mode and capacity of his spirit, rather than narrow them down to a meaning unadaptable to every palate. As a result, though we give some explanation of these stanzas, there is no reason to be bound to this explanation.[12]

The presence of the commentaries has had the effect

of imposing a meaning on the poems not discernible in the work of art itself. This is a pure example of the intentional fallacy–where we read not what the poet says but what we know, from other sources, he intends to say. No poet, perhaps, has been a victim of this literary heresy as has San Juan; no writer, perhaps, has presented his reader with such voluminous temptations. Even a reader who has read a small part or none of the commentaries normally assumes that his understanding of the poem is limited to the extent to which he does not possess the full explanations in the commentaries. At a high moment in the *Cántico* the poet writes:

> O birds on easy wings,
> lions, stags, leaping fallow deer,
> mountains, valleys, shores,
> waters, winds, passions
> and terror in the watchful nights.

He informs us in the commentaries that "waters denote the emotions of sorrow which afflict the soul, for they enter like water. David, referring to them, says to God: Salvum me fac, Deus, quoniam intraverunt aquae usque ad animam meam [Save me my God, for the waters have come in even unto my soul]. Ps 68:2." The birds, lions, stags, and leaping deer denote "the vicious and inordinate acts of the three faculties, memory, intellect, and will." The last two lines "indicate the four passions: sorrow, hope, joy, and fear." These are rather simple explanations, although here as elsewhere he then elaborates them extensively beyond the above outline. But they are not explanations apparent from the text alone.[13] Jorge Guillén comments on this particular stanza: "Strictly speaking it is a nonmystical poem, and irremediably so, for the ineffable experience and the theoretical mechanism both remain outside it."[14]

In short, while the commentaries depend on the poems, the poems do not depend on the commentaries and are often distorted by them; it is not necessary to know the commentaries in order to understand the poems. One can read them with pleasure but they are no more necessary to the autonomous poems than another author's commentaries on them might be.

If, then, we do not resort to the commentaries–which deal with only the central poems–can we discover a mystical message in these poems? Here we must hedge a bit, for is there a reader of San Juan de la Cruz who has not been forewarned to look for the mystical, even if he is unfamiliar with the commentaries? If we assume that most readers will come to San Juan with some fore-knowledge, it is fair to say that an intelligent reader can easily identify the stages of purgation, illumination, union, and peace in *Noche oscura,* and the union in *¡Oh Llama de amor viva!.* In *Cántico espiritual,* however, in either the first or the reshuffled version, he will find it virtually impossible to follow a single journey from purgation to peaceful beatitude.

While a reader *may* identify the stages of the mystical experience in *Noche oscura,* which is San Juan's most coherent allegory of it, he may also read the poem simply as an erotic love poem, where the lovers join in sexual union (the spiritual marriage) , a poem which because of its intense drama, beauty, and rapture brings us, at least emotionally, to a level of ecstasy which is implicit in the mystical experience. But this is secular, not religious, mysticism, if we must use the word "mysticism." In *Noche oscura,* perhaps the greatest of San Juan's poems, the text alone does not provide us with certain basic character-istics of the mystical experience, such as total self-detach-ment from the senses, a rising toward the godhead, a dying in life from time and space; these attributes are stated in the minor poems, some of which, as we have said, are explicitly mystical in their conceptual presenta-tion, and which can only be understood in this light. As an informed reader, I cannot read this poem without being aware of San Juan's mystical intention–the dark-ness and light are there and they enhance the total effect; at the same time the darkness, light, and union of lovers are presented so faithfully that *the immediate meaning of the words dominates their allegorical intent.* San Juan is not the only poet to give us something other than what he may have consciously intended. We may recall at once Blake's interpretation of Milton's Lucifer, whom he claims Milton unconsciously made his moral hero. *Noche oscura* is a glorification of human love in the same way that *¡Oh Llama de amor viva!* is an intimate description of sexual union and human tenderness and *Cántico* is a bright affirmation of the beauty of nature and of two lovers.

Until the present, San Juan has been interpreted almost exclusively on the basis of his biography and commentaries. When seeking a clarification of the text, it has been the practice to go outside the structure of the poem. One major dissenter, however, has been the poet Jorge Guillén, whose own life's work, *Cántico,* is an eloquent sign of his closeness to San Juan. Guillén writes:

> Although the mystic spirit thus imposes itself in the field of erotic images, the *Dark Night of the Soul,* the *Spiritual Canticle,* and the *Living Flame of Love* exist as a group of independent songs, or almost independent, with an almost complete coherence of metaphor, so continuous that it ceases to be metaphor and becomes the relating of adventures and exalting of emotions, especially in the *Dark Night* and the *Flame.* This brings us, then, to the conclusion that San Juan de la Cruz, the greatest of all the mystics, composed poems which it is customary to consider mystical for reasons that are biographical and allegorical, on the basis of a combined reading of the prose and poetry which superimposes the commentaries on the verses. Our purely poetic reading does not take anything away from the poems, which are indeed poems, and admirable ones, without biography or allegory. Their poetic value is not heightened by being turned toward the conceptual.[15]

In speaking of *Cántico espiritual,* he goes further:

> Strictly speaking, with complete theoretical rigor, they are not, they cannot be mystical. The almost

perfect autonomy of the images, so continuously referring to human love, admits neither the evocation of the experience, which is not conceivable or revealable, nor the interposing of thought upheld by allegorical scaffolding outside the poetic structure.[16]

The above arguments should not keep us from discovering the inner flame in San Juan, nor the profoundly metaphysical labyrinths of his poetry. But we must read his *poems* to discover the poet–and this lyric voice will be the true spiritual biography of the man. The case is comparable to that of Sappho, whose defenders until this day have uniformly insisted that we read her love poems to other women, not for what they say but as references to figures in a *thiasos* (a religious beauty cult) or as epithalamia written for ceremonial purposes.[17]

Both San Juan and Sappho are authors with poems in search of a reader. If San Juan's major poems are verse about the soul of man uniting with God, then his expression of it makes God the world, nature, and its creatures who love. He imposes perfection upon the things of this world, through his invisible skills as an artist, and affirms the beauty of lovers in darkness and flame, bringing them to the summit of ecstasy.

Tras de un amoroso lance,
y no de esperanza falto,
volé tan alto, tan alto,
que le di a la caza alcance.

Full of hope I climbed the day
while hunting the game of love,
and soared so high, high above
that at last I caught my prey.

TEXTS AND TRANSLATIONS

The problem of texts in San Juan is not nearly so grave as with most major poets of the period. There is no real certainty about capitalization and punctuation, but other doubtful readings are all minor. There is the matter of two versions of *Cántico espiritual*. The eleventh stanza is usually omitted from the first version, if the Sanlúcar codex is followed as it is here, and included in the second redaction based on the codex of Jaén. The general text for poems used in this edition is *Obras de San Juan de la Cruz*, ed. by P. Silverio de Santa Teresa, Burgos, 1929–31, 5 vols. A very convenient edition in English translation of prose, poetry, and letters is *The Collected Works of St. John of the Cross*, trans. Kavanaugh and Rodriguez, Doubleday, New York, 1964. It contains a much more readable translation of the commentaries than the E. Allison Peers versions. The most useful single-volume edition in Spanish is *Vida y Obras de San Juan de la Cruz*, Biblioteca de Autores Cristianos, Madrid, 1940; this edition also contains an extensive biography, fully documented, by the late Crisógono de Jesús.

In the text presented here the capitalization has been standardized, following modern practice. The titles in San Juan are a jungle, with almost no two texts presenting the same ones. By and large the titles were added later and are usually an interpolation borrowed from, and uniting the poems to, the commentaries. The traditional titles of *Noche oscura, Cántico espiritual, ¡Oh Llama de amor viva!, El pastorcico,* and *La fonte* are given; the remaining poems have first-line titles. Some of the profusion of variant titles are given in the appendix.

San Juan's nine *romances* (ballads) are not translated as poems. Because the *romances* are so markedly inferior to his other poems, their authenticity has been questioned. But there seems to be sufficient evidence to attribute them to him, and it appears that the first *romance* was the poem he dictated to the nuns the day of his escape from his prison cell in Toledo. I have not translated them as poems because I think I could not make them good poems in English; in Spanish they detract from rather than add to the poet's work, despite an occasional felicitous phrase. For the sake of completeness, however, they are given in the appendix with a prose translation. The hymn *Super flumina Babylonis* is a better poem; it is somewhat extravagant to attempt a verse translation into English of a Spanish translation from the Latin of an original poem in Hebrew. Included here is a very bare close version.

Finally, a word about the English version of San Juan's poetry. I wish to give no apologies–so much has been written about verse translation–but I do wish to make a few declarations. In some ways, all my life as a writer has been a preparation for these English versions: there is no poet, in regard to art and spirit, with whom I have felt such a constant affinity. His clarity, simplicity, and resonance are the qualities of language I would most like to see in an English version. In my own attempts *Noche oscura* has been my undoing. I think it the most complete poem in the Spanish language. I have made literally hundreds of versions, yet each change seems to cause as much loss as any possible gain; one meaning or sound fades as another appears. The first three lines have been for me impossible, making me wonder how I went beyond them.

NOTES

1. In the last year of his life, when he was being persecuted by authorities in his own order of Carmelites, we hear that the nuns of the convent of Beas de Segura, in northern Andalusia, destroyed all letters and papers of San Juan they had, out of fear that such material might be used as evidence against him or might implicate them. This was San Juan's favorite monastery, to which he returned many times. His friends among the nuns, we know, had been the impetus behind the writing of some of his commentaries. It is not unlikely that among all his papers destroyed were lines or poems which have not come down to us. In any case, it is scarcely conceivable that San Juan sprang, as it were, full grown into the world of letters, with no earlier poems.

2. Jorge Guillén, "The Ineffable Language of Mysticism: San Juan de la Cruz," *Language and Poetry*, Cambridge, Mass., Harvard University Press, 1961, p. 79.

3. Fray Juan had already been kidnapped once before, early in 1576, when the Calced Carmelites carried him off to Medina del Campo from the Convent of Encarnación at Avila.

4. Gerald Brenan, "Studies in Genius-II: St. John of the Cross, His Life and Poetry," *Horizon*, May 1947, p. 266.

5. *The Collected Works of St. John of the Cross,* trans. Kieran Kavanaugh and Otilio Rodriguez, New York, Doubleday, 1963, p. 685.

6. This poem is attributed to San Juan, although some doubt remains as to its authorship. It is normally included among his works in reliable texts.

7. When theological words such as "God" and "soul" are used in this introduction, the intention is to use a vocabulary corresponding to the intended public meaning of the poems. Their use is not meant to affirm the existence of God, the soul, the mystical experience, or anything supernatural. It should be added that neither the esthetic nor the intellectual impact of San Juan's poetry depends necessarily on a concordance of metaphysical beliefs between poet and reader.

8. There is some doubt about the authenticity of the Jaén redaction, doubts which most authorities have discounted. The commentaries are based on the second version.

9. *Spiritual Canticle,* St. John of the Cross, trans. E. Allison Peers, New York, Image Books, Doubleday, 1961, p. 40.

10. The term "minor poems" is customarily applied to poems other than *Cántico, Noche oscura,* and *¡Oh Llama de amor viva!,* the three central poems which are the subject of San Juan's extensive commentaries.

11. Kavanaugh and Rodriguez, p. 408. The Kavanaugh and Rodriguez translation is used here rather than the Peers for reasons of style. Peers's rendition of *figuras, comparaciones y semejanzas* as "figures, comparisons and similitudes" is more accurate, however, than "figures and similes," found in Kavanaugh and Rodriguez.

12. Ibid., p. 409.

13. Guillén, p. 111.

14. It should also be noted that San Juan's commentaries are on his second redaction of the poem *Cántico espiritual,* the doctrinal order which is normally considered inferior. San Juan wrote four voluminous books of commentaries: *The Spiritual Canticle, The Living Flame of Love, The Ascent of Mount Carmel,* and *The Black Night,* of which the latter two concern the poem *Noche oscura.* Although San Juan writes approximately 400 pages on the poem *Noche oscura,* his analysis of the text does not go beyond the third stanza of the eight-stanza poem.

15. Guillén, p. 115.

16. Ibid., p. 118.

17. For further discussion of the problem of text versus biography and history, see *Sappho: Lyrics in the Original Greek with Translations by Willis Barnstone,* New York, Anchor Books, Doubleday, 1965, pp. xxiv–xxviii.

THE
POEMS
OF
SAINT
JOHN
OF THE
CROSS

NOCHE OSCURA

En una noche oscura
con ansias en amores inflamada,
¡oh dichosa ventura!
salí sin ser notada,
estando ya mi casa sosegada.

A escuras, y segura
por la secreta escala disfrazada,
¡oh dichosa ventura!
a escuras, y en celada,
estando ya mi casa sosegada.

En la noche dichosa
en secreto, que nadie me veía
ni yo miraba cosa,
sin otra luz y guía,
sino la que en el corazón ardía.

Aquesta me guiaba
más cierto que la luz del mediodía,
a donde me esperaba,
quien yo bien me sabía,
en parte donde nadie parecía.

¡Oh noche, que guiaste!
¡Oh noche amable más que el alborada!
¡Oh noche que juntaste
amado con amada,
amada en el amado trasformada!

En mi pecho florido,
que entero para él sólo se guardaba,
allí quedó dormido,
y yo le regalaba,
y el ventalle de cedros aire daba.

DARK NIGHT

On a dark secret night,
starving for love and deep in flame,
O happy lucky flight!
unseen I slipped away,
my house at last was calm and safe.

Blackly free from light,
disguised and down a secret way,
O happy lucky flight!
in darkness I escaped,
my house at last was calm and safe.

On that happy night–in
secret; no one saw me through the dark–
and I saw nothing then,
no other light to mark
the way but fire pounding my heart.

That flaming guided me
more firmly than the noonday sun,
and waiting there was he
I knew so well–who shone
where nobody appeared to come.

O night, my guide!
O night more friendly than the dawn!
O tender night that tied
lover and the loved one,
loved one in the lover fused as one!

On my flowering breasts
which I had saved for him alone,
he slept and I caressed
and fondled him with love,
and cedars fanned the air above.

El aire de la almena,
cuando yo sus cabellos esparcía,
con su mano serena
en mi cuello hería,
y todos mis sentidos suspendía.

Quedéme, y olvidéme,
el rostro recliné sobre el amado,
cesó todo, y dejéme,
dejando mi cuidado
entre las azucenas olvidado.

Wind from the castle wall
while my fingers played in his hair:
  its hand serenely fell
  wounding my neck, and there
my senses vanished in the air.

  I lay. Forgot my being,
and on my love I leaned my face.
  All ceased. I left my being,
  leaving my cares to fade
among the lilies far away.

CÁNTICO ESPIRITUAL

(1st redaction, codex of Sanlúcar de Barrameda)

ESPOSA

¿A dónde te escondiste,
amado, y me dejaste con gemido?
como el ciervo huiste,
habiéndome herido;
salí tras tí clamando, y eras ido.

Pastores, los que fuerdes
allá por las majadas al otero,
si por ventura vierdes
aquel que yo más quiero,
decidle que adolezco, peno y muero.

Buscando mis amores,
iré por esos montes y riberas,
ni cogeré las flores,
ni temeré las fieras,
y pasaré los fuertes y fronteras.

PREGUNTA A LAS CRIATURAS

¡Oh bosques y espesuras,
plantadas por la mano del amado,
oh prado de verduras,
de flores esmaltado,
decid si por vosotros ha pasado!

RESPUESTA DE LAS CRIATURAS

Mil gracias derramando,
pasó por estos sotos con presura,
y yéndolos mirando,
con sola su figura
vestidos los dejó de hermosura.

BRIDE

Where have you hidden away?
You left me whimpering, my love.
Wounding me you vanished
like the stag. I rushed out
shouting for you–but you were gone.

O shepherds, you who climb
with your sheep high across the slope,
if by chance you see
the one I love most deeply,
tell him I suffer, grieve and die.

To find my love Ill go
along the riverbanks and mountains.
I shall not pick the flowers,
nor fear the prowling beasts;
Ill pass by fortress and frontier.

SHE ASKS THE CREATURES

O open woods and thickets
seeded by the lover's hand,
O meadow of green plants
enameled in bright flowers,
tell me if he has come your way.

THE CREATURES

Showering a thousand graces
he came hurriedly through these groves,
he looked at them and in
the radiance of his gaze
he left the woodland robed in beauty.

¡Ay, quién podrá sanarme!
Acaba de entregarte ya de vero,
no quieras enviarme
de hoy ya más mensajero,
que no saben decirme lo que quiero.

Y todos cuantos vagan,
de ti me van mil gracias refiriendo
y todos más me llagan,
y déjame muriendo
un no sé qué que quedan balbuciendo.

Mas ¿cómo perseveras,
oh vida, no viviendo donde vives,
y haciendo porque mueras,
las flechas que recibes,
de lo que del amado en ti concibes?

¿Por qué, pues has llagado
a aqueste corazón, no le sanaste?
Y pues me le has robado,
¿por qué así le dejaste,
y no tomas el robo que robaste?

Apaga mis enojos,
pues que ninguno basta a deshacellos,
y véante mis ojos,
pues eres lumbre dellos,
y sólo para ti quiero tenellos.

Descubre tu presencia,
y máteme tu vista y hermosura:
mira que la dolencia
de amor, que no se cura
sino con la presencia y la figura.*

* This stanza is not included in the codex of Sanlúcar de
Barrameda, but in that of Jaén. It is added here, however. Even in

BRIDE

O who can heal my wound!
Quickly, surrender to me now.
    As of today, please send
    me no more messengers
who cannot tell me what I want.

    All those who wander here
inform me of your thousand graces,
    yet each word is a blow,
    and they keep babbling bits
of mystery–leaving me near death.

    And how do you go on,
O life, not living where you live,
    when arrows from the lover,
    which are conceived in you,
fly deep in you–making you die?

    Why do you wound my heart
and then refuse to make it heal?
    And since you took it from me,
    why do you leave it now,
abandoning the thing you robbed?

    Let my sufferings cease
for there is no one who can cure them;
    let my eyes see your face,
    you are their only light;
for you alone I care for them.

    Reveal your presence to me
and kill me by your gaze and beauty.
    See how the suffering
    of love is only cured
when you–or when your face–is near.

most editions following the order of Sanlúcar, the stanza is included
since it is authentic.

[45]

¡Oh cristalina fuente,
si en esos tus semblantes plateados,
formases de repente
los ojos deseados,
que tengo en mis entrañas dibujados!

Apártalos, amado,
que voy de vuelo.

ESPOSO

Vuélvete, paloma,
que el ciervo vulnerado
por el otero asoma,
al aire de tu vuelo, y fresco toma.

ESPOSA

Mi amado, las montañas,
los valles solitarios nemorosos,
las ínsulas extrañas,
los ríos sonorosos,
el silbo de los aires amorosos.

La noche sosegada
en par de los levantes de la aurora,
la música callada,
la soledad sonora,
la cena que recrea y enamora.

Nuestro lecho florido,
de cuevas de leones enlazado,
en púrpura tendido,
de paz edificado,
de mil escudos de oro coronado.

A zaga de tu huella
las jóvenes discurren al camino
al toque de centella,
al adobado vino,
emisiones de bálsamo divino.

O crystal brook, if on
the silver surface of the water
    you instantly might form
    the eyes I most desire!
I feel them in me like a scar!

Look away, my love,
Im going to fly.

BRIDEGROOM
                My dove, turn back,
for now the wounded stag
is climbing up the slope,
freshened by the breeze of your flight.

BRIDE
My love, the mountains and
the solitary wooded valleys,
    the unexpected islands,
    the loud sonorous rivers,
the whistling of the loving winds.

The night of total calm
before the rising winds of dawn,
    the music of a silence,
    the sounding solitude,
the supper that renews our love.

Our flowery bed is safely
hidden among the lion caves,
    under a purple tent
    erected in deep peace
and capped with thousands of gold shields.

Young girls wander about
the roads seeking a sign from you
    in the falling lightning
    or in the scented wine
which emanates a holy balm.

En la interior bodega
de mi amado bebí, y cuando salía
por toda aquesta vega,
ya cosa no sabía,
y el ganado perdí, que antes seguía.

Allí me dio su pecho,
allí me enseñó ciencia muy sabrosa,
y yo le di de hecho
a mí, sin dejar cosa;
allí le prometí de ser su esposa.

Mi alma se ha empleado,
y todo mi caudal en su servicio:
ya no guardo ganado,
ni ya tengo otro oficio;
que ya sólo en amar es mi ejercicio.

Pues ya si en el ejido,
de hoy más no fuere vista ni hallada,
diréis que me he perdido,
que andando enamorada,
me hice perdidiza, y fui ganada.

De flores y esmeraldas
en las frescas mañanas escogidas,
haremos las guirnaldas,
en tu amor florecidas,
y en un cabello mío entretejidas.

En sólo aquel cabello,
que en mi cuello volar consideraste,
mirástele en mi cuello,
y en él preso quedaste,
y en uno de mis ojos te llagaste.

Cuando tú me mirabas,
tu gracia en mí tus ojos imprimían:
por eso me adamabas,
y en eso merecían
los míos adorar lo que en ti vían.

Deep in the winevault of
my love I drank, and when I came
out on this open meadow
I knew no thing at all,
I lost the flock I used to drive.

He held me to his chest
and taught me a sweet science. In-
stantly I yielded all
I had–keeping nothing–
and promised then to be his bride.

I gave my soul to him
and all the things I owned were his:
I have no flock to tend
nor any other trade
and my one ministry is love.

If Im no longer seen
following sheep about the hills,
say that I am lost, that
wandering in love I let
myself be lost and then was won.

On cool mornings we shall
find emeralds and flowers, and make
a garland for your hair,
blossoming in your love
and then looped in a lock of mine.

You stared at that one lock
of windblown hair you saw against
my nape, and on my neck
you were a prisoner
gashing yourself in one of my eyes.

When first you looked my way
your eyes printed your grace in me
and made me feel a woman,
and so my eyes could love
all things which they observed in you.

[49]

No quieras despreciarme,
que si color moreno en mí hallaste,
ya bien puedes mirarme,
después que me miraste,
que gracia y hermosura en mí dejaste.

Cojednos las raposas,
que está ya florecida nuestra viña,
en tanto que de rosas
hacemos una piña,
y no parezca nadie en la montiña.

Detente, cierzo muerto;
ven, austro, que recuerdas los amores,
aspira por mi huerto,
y corran sus olores,
y pacerá el amado entre las flores.

ESPOSO
Entrádose ha la esposa
en el ameno huerto deseado,
y a su sabor reposa,
el cuello reclinado
sobre los dulces brazos del amado.

Debajo del manzano,
allí conmigo fuiste desposada,
allí te di la mano,
y fuiste reparada,
donde tu madre fuera violada.

A las aves ligeras,
leones, ciervos, gamos saltadores,
montes, valles, riberas,
aguas, aires, ardores,
y miedos de las noches veladores.

Do not despise me if
you find the color of my flesh
    is brown. Look at me well,
    and then see how you
endowed me with your grace and beauty.

    Catch us the little foxes,
our vines already are in bloom;
    while we take a handful of
    the roses for our spray
let no one in the hills appear.

    Stop, north wind of death
and come, south wind recalling love.
    Breathe on my garden, let
    aromas swell the air,
my love will graze among the flowers.

    BRIDEGROOM
    My bride has gone into
the pleasant garden she desired,
    and lies upon the grass
    happy, resting her neck
in the gentle arms of her love.

    Under the apple tree
you came and were engaged to me;
    there I gave you my hand
    and you were then redeemed
where once your mother had been raped.

    O birds on easy wings,
lions, stags, leaping fallow deer,
    mountains, valleys, shores,
    waters, winds, passions
and terror in the watchful nights.

Por las amenas liras
y canto de serenas os conjuro
que cesen vuestras iras,
y no toquéis al muro,
porque la esposa duerma más seguro.

ESPOSA
¡Oh ninfas de Judea,
en tanto que en las flores y rosales
el ámbar perfumea,
morá en los arrabales,
y no queráis tocar nuestros umbrales!

Escóndete, carillo,
y mira con tu haz a las montañas,
y no quieras decillo;
mas mira las compañas
de la que va por ínsulas extrañas.

ESPOSO
La blanca palomica
al arca con el ramo se ha tornado,
y ya la tortolica
al socio deseado
en las riberas verdes ha hallado.

En soledad vivía,
y en soledad ha puesto ya su nido,
y en soledad la guía
a solas su querido,
también en soledad de amor herido.

ESPOSA
Gocémonos, amado,
y vámonos a ver en tu hermosura
al monte o al collado,
do mana el agua pura;
entremos más adentro en la espesura.

With the song of the sirens
and graceful harp, I ask you now
to put an end to anger
and not to touch the wall
so that the bride may sleep in peace.

BRIDE

O virgins of Judea,
while the perfume of amber hangs
on flowers and the rose tree,
live in some far-off place
and dont appear before our door!

Hide, my darling, and turn
your face to look upon the mountains,
and dont tell what you know
but look at friends of her
who goes to legendary islands.

BRIDEGROOM

The white tiny dove
flew to the Ark carrying a frond
and now the turtledove
has come upon her mate
on the green borders of the river.

She lived in solitude,
in solitude she made her nest
and all alone her lover
led her in solitude,
wounded in solitude by love.

BRIDE

Let us be happy, darling,
and see us mirrored in your beauty
on mountains and the hills
where limpid waters plash;
let us go deeper in the wood.

Y luego a las subidas
cavernas de la piedra nos iremos,
que están bien escondidas,
y allí nos entraremos,
y el mosto de granadas gustaremos.

Allí me mostrarías
aquello que mi alma pretendía
y luego me darías
allí tú, vida mía,
aquello que me diste el otro día.

El aspirar del aire,
el canto de la dulce filomena,
el soto y su donaire,
en la noche serena
con llama que consume y no da pena.

Que nadie lo miraba,
Aminadab tampoco parecía,
y el cerco sosegaba,
y la caballería
a vista de las aguas descendía.

And then we'll climb high, high
to peaks riddled with stony caves
    safely hidden away,
    and there we'll go inside
and taste the pomegranate wine.

    There you will reveal
to me the things my soul desired,
    and in a flash, O love,
    there you will restore
what but a day ago you gave to me.

    The breathing of the air,
song of a tender nightingale,
    the fresh exquisite grove,
    serene and secret night
of flame that burns and gives no pain.

    No one was looking there,
no shadow of Aminadab;
    the siege was quieted,
    and then before the waters
the cavalry descended into view.

¡OH LLAMA DE AMOR VIVA!

¡Oh llama de amor viva,
que tiernamente hieres
de mi alma en el más profundo centro!
Pues ya no eres esquiva,
acaba ya si quieres,
rompe la tela deste dulce encuentro.

¡Oh cauterio suave!
¡Oh regalada llaga!
¡Oh mano blanda! ¡Oh toque delicado,
que a vida eterna sabe,
y toda deuda paga!
Matando, muerte en vida la has trocado.

¡Oh lámparas de fuego,
en cuyos resplandores
las profundas cavernas del sentido,
que estaba oscuro y ciego,
con extraños primores
calor y luz dan junto a su querido!

¡Cuán manso y amoroso
recuerdas en mi seno,
donde secretamente sólo moras:
y en tu aspirar sabroso
de bien y gloria lleno
cuán delicadamente me enamoras!

O LIVING FLAME OF LOVE!

O living flame of love,
how tenderly you wound
my soul in her profoundest core!
You are no longer shy.
Do it now, I ask you:
break the membrane of our sweet union.

O soothing cautery!
O wound that is a joy!
O gentle hand! O delicate touch
tasting of eternity,
repaying every debt.
Killing, you turn my death to life.

O lamps of human fire,
in deep transparency
the lowest caverns of the senses,
once shadowy and blind,
flare in light and warmth
and wake the lover with amazing joy!

How lovingly and soft
you make my breasts recall
where you alone lie secretly;
and with your honeyed breath,
replete with grace and glory,
how tenderly you make me love!

Entréme donde no supe
y quedéme no sabiendo,
toda ciencia trascendiendo.

Yo no supe dónde entraba,
pero, cuando allí me vi,
sin saber dónde me estaba,
grandes cosas entendí;
no diré lo que sentí,
que me quedé no sabiendo,
toda ciencia trascendiendo.

De paz y de piedad
era la ciencia perfecta,
en profunda soledad,
entendida vía recta;
era cosa tan secreta,
que me quedé balbuciendo,
toda ciencia trascendiendo.

Estaba tan embebido,
tan absorto y ajenado,
que se quedó mi sentido
de todo sentir privado;
y el espíritu dotado
de un entender no entendiendo,
toda ciencia trascendiendo.

El que allí llega de vero,
de sí mismo desfallesce;
cuanto sabía primero
mucho bajo le paresce;
y su ciencia tanto cresce,
que se queda no sabiendo,
toda ciencia trascendiendo.

I CAME INTO THE UNKNOWN

I came into the unknown
and stayed there unknowing,
rising beyond all science.*

I did not know the door
but when I found the way,
unknowing where I was,
I learned enormous things,
but what I felt I cannot say,
for I remained unknowing,
rising beyond all science.

It was the perfect realm
of holiness and peace.
In deepest solitude
I found the narrow way:
a secret giving such release
that I was stunned and stammering,
rising beyond all science.

I was so far inside,
so dazed and far away
my senses were released
from feelings of my own.
My mind had found a surer way:
a knowledge by unknowing,
rising beyond all science.

And he who does arrive
collapses as in sleep,
for all he knew before
now seems a lowly thing,
and so his knowledge grows so deep
that he remains unknowing,
rising beyond all science.

* *science:* used in primary sense, in Spanish and English, of
systematized knowledge.

Cuanto más alto se sube,
tanto menos entendía
que es la tenebrosa nube
que a la noche esclarecía;
por eso quien la sabía
queda siempre no sabiendo
toda ciencia trascendiendo.

Este saber no sabiendo
es de tan alto poder,
que los sabios arguyendo
jamás le pueden vencer;
que no llega su saber
a no entender entendiendo,
toda ciencia trascendiendo.

Y es de tan alta excelencia
aqueste sumo saber,
que no hay facultad ni ciencia
que le puedan emprender;
quien se supiere vencer
con un no saber sabiendo,
irá siempre trascendiendo.

Y si lo queréis oir,
consiste esta suma ciencia
en un subido sentir
de la divinal Esencia;
es obra de su clemencia
hacer quedar no entendiendo,
toda ciencia trascendiendo.

The higher he ascends
the darker is the wood;
it is the shadowy cloud
that clarified the night,
and so the one who understood
remains always unknowing,
rising beyond all science.

This knowledge by unknowing
is such a soaring force
that scholars argue long
but never leave the ground.
Their knowledge always fails the source:
to understand unknowing,
rising beyond all science.

This knowledge is supreme
crossing a blazing height;
though formal reason tries
it crumbles in the dark,
but one who would control the night
by knowledge of unknowing
will rise beyond all science.

And if you wish to hear:
the highest science leads
to an ecstatic feeling
of the most holy Being;
and from his mercy comes his deed:
to let us stay unknowing,
rising beyond all science.

VIVO SIN VIVIR EN MÍ

Vivo sin vivir en mí,
y de tal manera espero,
que muero porque no muero.

En mí yo no vivo ya,
y sin Dios vivir no puedo;
pues sin él y sin mí quedo,
este vivir ¿qué será?
Mil muertes se me hará,
pues mi misma vida espero,
muriendo porque no muero.

Esta vida que yo vivo
es privación de vivir;
y así, es contino morir
hasta que viva contigo;
oye, mi Dios, lo que digo,
que esta vida no la quiero;
que muero porque no muero.

Estando absente de tí,
¿qué vida puedo tener,
sino muerte padescer,
la mayor que nunca vi?
Lástima tengo de mí,
pues de suerte persevero,
que muero porque no muero.

El pez que del agua sale,
aun de alivio no caresce,
que en la muerte que padesce,
al fin la muerte le vale;
¿qué muerte habrá que se iguale
a mi vivir lastimero,
pues si más vivo más muero?

I LIVE YET DO NOT LIVE IN ME

I live yet do not live in me,
am waiting as my life goes by,
and die because I do not die.

No longer do I live in me,
and without God I cannot live;
to him or me I cannot give
my self, so what can living be?
A thousand deaths my agony
waiting as my life goes by,
dying because I do not die.

This life I live alone I view
as robbery of life, and so
it is a constant death–with no
way out until I live with you.
God, hear me, what I say is true:
I do not want this life of mine,
and die because I do not die.

Being so removed from you I say
what kind of life can I have here
but death so ugly and severe
and worse than any form of pain?
I pity me–and yet my fate
is that I must keep up this lie,
and die because I do not die.

The fish taken out of the sea
is not without a consolation:
his dying is of brief duration
and ultimately brings relief.
Yet what convulsive death can be
as bad as my pathetic life?
The more I live the more I die.

Cuando me pienso aliviar
de verte en el Sacramento,
háceme más sentimiento
el no te poder gozar;
todo es para más pensar,
por no verte como quiero,
y muero porque no muero.

Y si me gozo, Señor,
con esperanza de verte,
en ver que puedo perderte
se me dobla mi dolor;
viviendo en tanto pavor,
y esperando como espero,
muérome porque no muero.

Sácame de aquesta muerte,
mi Dios, y dame la vida;
no me tengas impedida
en este lazo tan fuerte;
mira que peno por verte,
y mi mal es tan entero,
que muero porque no muero.

Lloraré mi muerte ya,
y lamentaré mi vida
en tanto que detenida
por mis pecados está.
¡Oh mi Dios! ¿cuando será?
cuando yo diga de vero:
vivo ya porque no muero.

When I begin to feel relief
on seeing you in the sacrament,
I sink in deeper discontent,
deprived of your sweet company.
Now everything compels my grief:
I want—yet cant—see you nearby,
and die because I do not die.

Although I find my pleasure, Sir,
in hope of someday seeing you,
I see that I can lose you too,
which makes my pain doubly severe,
and so I live in darkest fear,
and hope, wait as life goes by,
dying because I do not die.

Deliver me from death, my God,
and give me life; now you have wound
a rope about me; harshly bound
I ask you to release the cord.
See how I die to see you, Lord,
and I am shattered where I lie,
dying because I do not die.

My death will trigger tears in me,
and I shall mourn my life: a day
annihilated by the way
I fail and sin relentlessly.
O Father God, when will it be
that I can say without a lie:
I live because I do not die?

Tras de un amoroso lance,
y no de esperanza falto,
volé tan alto, tan alto,
que le di a la caza alcance.

Para que yo alcance diese
a aqueste lance divino,
tanto volar me convino
que de vista me perdiese;
y con todo, en este trance,
en el vuelo quedé falto;
mas el amor fue tan alto,
que le di a la caza alcance.

Cuando más alto subía,
deslumbróseme la vista,
y la más fuerte conquista
en escuro se hacía;
mas por ser de amor el lance
di un ciego y oscuro salto,
y fui tan alto, tan alto,
que le di a la caza alcance.

Cuanto más alto llegaba
de este lance tan subido,
tanto más bajo y rendido
y abatido me hallaba;
dije: No habrá quien alcance;
y abatíme tanto, tanto,
que fui tan alto, tan alto,
que le di a la caza alcance.

Por una extraña manera
mil vuelos pasé de un vuelo,
porque esperanza de cielo
tanto alcanza cuanto espera;

FULL OF HOPE I CLIMBED THE DAY

Full of hope I climbed the day
while hunting the game of love,
and soared so high, high above
that at last I caught my prey.

In order to seize the game
–the divine love in the sky–
I had to fly so high, high
I floated unseen and became
lost in that dangerous day;
and so my flight fell short of
height–yet so high was my love
that at last I caught my prey.

Dazzled and stunned by light
as I rose nearer the sun,
my greatest conquest was won
in the very black of night.
Yet since love opened my way
I leapt dark, blindly above
and was so high, near my love,
that at last I caught my prey.

In this most exalted quest
the higher I began to soar
the lower I felt–more sore
and broken and depressed.
I said: None can seize the prey!
and groveled so low, so low
that high, higher did I go,
and at last I caught my prey.

By strange reckoning I saw
a thousand flights in one flight;
for hope of heavenly light
is achieved by hoping now.

esperé sólo este lance,
y en esperar no fui falto,
pues fui tan alto, tan alto,
que le di a la caza alcance.

I hoped only for this way
and was right to wait for love,
and climbed so high, high above
that at last I caught my prey.

EL PASTORCICO

Un pastorcico solo está penado,
  ajeno de placer y de contento,
  y en su pastora puesto el pensamiento,
  y el pecho del amor muy lastimado.
No llora por haberle amor llagado,
  que no le pena verse así afligido,
  aunque en el corazón está herido;
  mas llora por pensar que está olvidado.

Que sólo de pensar que está olvidado
  de su bella pastora, con gran pena
  se deja maltratar en tierra ajena,
  el pecho del amor muy lastimado.
Y dice el pastorcico: ¡Ay, desdichado
  de aquel que de mi amor ha hecho ausencia,
  y no quiere gozar la mi presencia,
  y el pecho por su amor muy lastimado!

Y a cabo de un gran rato se ha encumbrado
  sobre un árbol do abrió sus brazos bellos,
  y muerto se ha quedado, asido de ellos,
  el pecho del amor muy lastimado.

THE YOUNG SHEPHERD

A young shepherd is alone and grave,
    alien to joy and happiness,
    and thinking of his shepherdess
    his heart is sorely hurt by love.
    He doesnt weep at being lost
    in love or wakening to pain,
    although his heart is sorely maimed;
    he weeps thinking he is forgot.

Merely the thought that his sweet friend
    forgot him is a painful sword;
    letting himself be hurt abroad
    his wounds of love can never end.
    The shepherd cries: O misery of
    her distance from my love, and she
    no longer cares to be near me!
    My heart is sorely hurt by love!

A long time passed: he climbed the branches of
    a tree and spread his lovely arms,
    and dead lay hanging from his arms;
    his heart was sorely hurt by love.

LA FONTE

Que bien sé yo la fonte que mana y corre,
aunque es de noche.

Aquella eterna fonte está ascondida,
que bien sé yo do tiene su manida,
aunque es de noche.

Su origen no lo sé, pues no le tiene,
mas sé que todo origen de ella viene,
aunque es de noche.

Sé que no puede ser cosa tan bella,
y que cielos y tierra beben de ella,
aunque es de noche.

Bien sé que suelo en ella no se halla,
y que ninguno puede vadealla,
aunque es de noche.

Su claridad nunca es escurecida,
y sé que toda luz de ella es venida,
aunque es de noche.

Sé ser tan caudalosas sus corrientes,
que infiernos, cielos riegan, y las gentes,
aunque es de noche.

El corriente que nace de esta fuente,
bien sé que es tan capaz y omnipotente,
aunque es de noche.

El corriente que de estas dos procede
sé que ninguna de ellas le precede,
aunque es de noche.

Aquesta eterna fonte está ascondida
en este vivo pan por darnos vida,
aunque es de noche.

THE FOUNTAIN

How well I know that flowing spring
   in black of night.

The eternal fountain is unseen.
How well I know where she has been
   in black of night.

I do not know her origin.
None. Yet in her all things begin
   in black of night.

I know that nothing is so fair
and earth and firmament drink there
   in black of night.

I know that none can wade inside
to find her bright bottomless tide
   in black of night.

Her shining never has a blur;
I know that all light comes from her
   in black of night.

I know her streams converge and swell
and nourish people, skies and hell
   in black of night.

The stream whose birth is in this source
I know has a gigantic force
   in black of night.

The stream from but these two proceeds
yet neither one, I know, precedes
   in black of night.

The eternal fountain is unseen
in living bread that gives us being
   in black of night.

Aquí se está llamando a las criaturas,
y de esta agua se hartan, aunque a escuras,
porque es de noche.

Aquesta viva fuente que deseo,
en este pan de vida yo la veo,
aunque de noche.

She calls on all mankind to start
to drink her water, though in dark,
   for black is night.

O living fountain that I crave,
in bread of life I see her flame
   in black of night.

Encima de las corrientes,
que en Babilonia hallaba,
allí me senté llorando,
allí la tierra regaba.

Acordándome de ti,
¡oh Sión! a quien amaba,
era dulce tu memoria,
y con ella más lloraba.

Dejé los trajes de fiesta,
los de trabajo tomaba,
y colgué en los verdes sauces
la música que llevaba,

poniéndola en esperanza
de aquello que en ti esperaba;
allí me hirió el amor,
y el corazón me sacaba.

Díjele que me matase,
pues de tal suerte llagaba:
yo me metía en su fuego,
sabiendo que me abrasaba,

desculpando el avecica
que en el fuego se acababa;
estábame en mí muriendo,
y en ti sólo respiraba.

En mí por ti me moría,
y por ti resucitaba,
que la memoria de ti
daba vida y la quitaba.

BY THE WATERS OF BABYLON

(based on Psalm 136)

By the waters of Babylon
I sat down and wept,
and my tears
watered the ground,

remembering you,
O Zion, whom I loved.
Your memory was sweet
and I wept more.

I took off holiday robes,
put on working clothes,
and hung my harp
on a green willow,

laying it there in hope
of the hope I had in you.
There love wounded me
and took away my heart.

I asked it to kill me
since it had stabbed me so.
I leaped into its fire
knowing it would burn me,

and forgave the young bird
dying in the fire.
I was dying in myself
and breathing only in you.

I died within for you
and for you I revived;
your memory
gave and took away life.

Gozábanse los extraños
entre quien cautivo estaba.

Preguntábanme cantares
de lo que en Sión cantaba:
Canta de Sión un himno,
veámos como sonaba.

Decid: ¿Cómo en tierra ajena,
donde por Sión lloraba,

cantaré yo la alegría
que en Sión se me quedaba?
Echaríala en olvido
si en la ajena me gozaba.

Con mi paladar se junte
la lengua con que hablaba,
si de ti yo me olvidare,
en la tierra do moraba.

Sión, por los verdes ramos
que Babilonia me daba,
de mí se olvide mi diestra,
que es lo que en ti más amaba,

si de ti no me acordare,
en lo que más me gozaba,
y si yo tuviese fiesta,
y sin ti la festejaba.

¡Oh hija de Babilonia,
mísera y desventurada!

bienaventurado era
aquel en quien confiaba,
que te ha de dar el castigo
que de tu mano llevaba.

Those strangers were glad,
they who were my captors,

and asked me to sing
what I sang in Zion:
"Sing us a hymn from Zion,
let us hear the song!"

I said how can I sing
in a foreign land where I weep,

how can I sing of joy
I felt in Zion.
I would be forgetting her,
if happy in a strange land.

May the tongue I speak with
cling to my palate
if I forget you
in this land where I am.

Zion, by the green branches
that Babylon gave me,
let my right arm be forgotten
(which I cared for
only when I was with you)

if I do not remember you
who made me happy,
or celebrate a day
from which you are gone.

O daughter of Babylon,
in misery and doomed!

I trusted him
who came blessed,
who will punish you
with your own hand.

Y juntará sus pequeños,
y a mí, porque en ti lloraba,
a la piedra que era Cristo,
por el cual yo te dejaba.*

* A last line is added to some copies: *Debetur soli gloria vera Deo*
[To God alone (is due) true glory].

He will bring his little ones
to me; he wept for you
at the rock which is Christ.
I left you for him.

Sin arrimo y con arrimo,
sin luz y a oscuras viviendo,
todo me voy consumiendo.

Mi alma está desasida
de toda cosa criada,
y sobre sí levantada,
y en una sabrosa vida,
sólo en su Dios arrimada;
por eso ya se dirá
la cosa que más estimo,
que mi alma se ve ya
sin arrimo y con arrimo.

Y aunque tinieblas padezco
en esta vida mortal,
no es tan crecido mi mal,
porque, si de luz carezco,
tengo vida celestial;
porque el amor de tal vida,
cuando más ciego va siendo,
que tiene el alma rendida,
sin luz y a oscuras viviendo.

Hace tal obra el amor,
después que le conocí,
que, si hay bien o mal en mí,
todo lo hace de un sabor,
y al alma transforma en sí;
y así en su llama sabrosa,
la cual en mí estoy sintiendo,
apriesa, sin quedar cosa,
todo me voy consumiendo.

WITHOUT A PLACE AND WITH A PLACE

Without a place and with a place
to rest–living darkly with no ray
of light–I burn my self away.

My soul–no longer bound–is free
from the creations of the world;
above itself it rises hurled
into a life of ecstasy,
leaning only on God. The world
will therefore clarify at last
what I esteem of highest grace:
my soul revealing it can rest
without a place and with a place.

Although I suffer a dark night
in mortal life, I also know
my agony is slight, for though
I am in darkness without light,
a clear heavenly life I know;
for love gives power to my life,
however black and blind my day,
to yield my soul, and free of strife
to rest–living darkly with no ray.

Love can perform a wondrous labor
which I have learned internally,
and all the good or bad in me
takes on a penetrating savor,
changing my soul so it can be
consumed in a delicious flame.
I feel it in me as a ray;
and quickly killing every trace
of light–I burn my self away.

POR TODA LA HERMOSURA

Por toda la hermosura
nunca yo me perderé,
sino por un no sé qué
que se alcanza por ventura.

Sabor de bien que es finito
lo más que puede llegar
es cansar el apetito
y estragar el paladar;
y así, por toda dulzura
nunca yo me perderé,
sino por un no sé qué
que se halla por ventura.

El corazón generoso
nunca cura de parar
donde se puede pasar,
sino en más dificultoso;
nada le causa hartura,
y sube tanto su fe,
que gusta de un no sé qué
que se halla por ventura.

El que de amor adolesce,
del divino ser tocado,
tiene el gusto tan trocado,
que a los gustos desfallesce;
como al que con calentura
fastidia el manjar que ve,
y apetece un no sé qué
que se halla por ventura.

No os maravilléis de aquesto,
que el gusto se quede tal,
porque es la causa del mal
ajena de todo el resto;

FOR ALL THE BEAUTY THERE MAY BE

For all the beauty there may be
Ill never throw away my soul;
only for something I dont know
that one may come on randomly.

In savoring a finite joy
the very most one can expect
is to enfeeble and destroy
our taste, leaving the palate wrecked;
for all the sweetness there may be
Ill never throw away my soul;
only for something I dont know
that one may come on randomly.

A generous heart will never care
to go part way; it wont be cowed
if there is passage anywhere,
but set out on the hardest road;
nothing can cause it misery,
and with faith soaring like a cloud
it feeds on something I dont know
that one may come on randomly.

One who suffers the pains of love
from contact with the holy being
will find himself abandoning
old tastes and killing remnants of
all taste–like one who feverishly
rejects the food he sees, although
he longs for something I dont know
that he may come on randomly.

Dont be surprised by all of this,
and let your taste remain as dead
for it will lead you to a bed
of evil far from any bliss;

y así, toda criatura
enajenada se ve,
y gusta de un no sé qué
que se halla por ventura.

Que estando la voluntad
de divinidad tocada,
no puede quedar pagada
sino con divinidad;
mas, por ser tal su hermosura,
que sólo se ve por fe,
gústala en un no sé qué
que se halla por ventura.

Pues de tal enamorado,
decidme si habréis dolor,
pues que no tiene sabor
entre todo lo criado;
solo, sin forma y figura,
sin hallar arrimo y pie,
gustando allá un no sé qué
que se halla por ventura.

No penséis que el interior,
que es de mucha más valía,
halla gozo y alegría
en lo que acá da sabor;
mas sobre toda hermosura,
y lo que es, y será y fue,
gusta de allá un no sé qué
que se halla por ventura.

Más emplea su cuidado,
quien se quiere aventajar,
en lo que está por ganar,
que en lo que tiene ganado;
y así, para más altura
yo siempre me inclinaré
sobre todo a un no sé qué
que se halla por ventura.

for every living being is seen
to be relentlessly alone
and feeds on something I dont know
that he may come on randomly.

And once the will has felt the mark
of the divinity, it can-
not be repaid by any man;
only the Lord can heal the dark;
His beauty is of such degree
as to be seen through faith alone,
tasted in something I dont know
that one may come on randomly.

With such a lover as the Lord
tell me if you will be in pain,
for His love is devoid of taste
among the things made in this world.
Without a foothold you must seek
Him out—no face nor form, alone—
tasting there something I dont know
that one may come on randomly.

And dont look to your inner eye
(though of a vastly greater worth)
to find among the joys of earth
a happiness and ecstasy;
more than all beauty there may be
or may have been or can be now,
one feeds on something I dont know
that one may come on randomly.

Whoever cares to do his best
should look for what may still be gained,
not what already is obtained,
and he will see the higher crest.
And so to reach the utmost peak
I always shall be moved to go
largely to something I dont know
that one may come on randomly.

Por lo que por el sentido
puede acá comprehenderse,
y todo lo que entenderse,
aunque sea muy subido,
ni por gracia y hermosura
yo nunca me perderé,
sino por un no sé qué
que se halla por ventura.

On earth you never must rely
on what the senses understand
or all the knowledge you command,
although it rises very high.
No grace nor beauty there may be
will make me throw away my soul;
only for something I dont know
that one may come on randomly.

DEL VERBO DIVINO

Del Verbo divino
la Virgen preñada
viene de camino
si le dais posada.

SUMA DE LA PERFECCIÓN

Olvido de lo criado,
memoria del Criador,
atención a lo interior
y estarse amando al Amado.

·OF THE DIVINE WORD

Pregnant with the holy
Word will come the Virgin
walking down the road
if you will take her in.

PEAK OF PERFECTION

All things of the Maker
forgotten–but not Him;
exploration within,
and loving the Lover.

CÁNTICO ESPIRITUAL

(2nd redaction, codex of Jaén)

ESPOSA

¿A dónde te escondiste,
amado, y me dejaste con gemido?
como el ciervo huiste,
habiéndome herido;
salí tras tí clamando, y eras ido.

Pastores, los que fuerdes
allá por las majadas al otero,
si por ventura vierdes
aquel que yo más quiero,
decidle que adolezco, peno y muero.

Buscando mis amores,
iré por esos montes y riberas,
ni cogeré las flores,
ni temeré las fieras,
y pasaré los fuertes y fronteras.

PREGUNTA A LAS CRIATURAS

¡Oh bosques y espesuras,
plantadas por la mano del amado,
oh prado de verduras,
de flores esmaltado,
decid si por vosotros ha pasado!

RESPUESTA DE LAS CRIATURAS

Mil gracias derramando,
pasó por estos sotos con presura,
y yéndolos mirando,
con sola su figura
vestidos los dejó de hermosura.

BRIDE

Where have you hidden away?
You left me whimpering, my love.
Wounding me you vanished
like the stag. I rushed out
shouting for you–but you were gone.

O shepherds, you who climb
with your sheep high across the slope,
if by some chance you see
the one I love most deeply,
tell him I suffer, grieve and die.

To find my love Ill go
along the riverbanks and mountains.
I shall not pick the flowers,
nor fear the prowling beasts;
Ill pass by fortress and frontier.

SHE ASKS THE CREATURES

O open woods and thickets
seeded by the lover's hand,
O meadow of green plants
enameled in bright flowers,
tell me if he has come your way.

THE CREATURES

Showering a thousand graces
he came hurriedly through these groves,
he looked at them and in
the radiance of his gaze
he left the woodland robed in beauty.

ESPOSA

¡Ay, quién podrá sanarme!
Acaba de entregarte ya de vero,
no quieras enviarme
de hoy ya más mensajero,
que no saben decirme lo que quiero.

Y todos cuantos vagan,
de ti me van mil gracias refiriendo
y todos más me llagan,
y déjame muriendo
un no sé qué que quedan balbuciendo.

Mas ¿cómo perseveras,
oh vida, no viviendo donde vives,
y haciendo porque mueras,
las flechas que recibes,
de lo que del amado en ti concibes?

¿Por qué, pues has llagado
a aqueste corazón, no le sanaste?
Y pues me le has robado,
¿por qué así le dejaste,
y no tomas el robo que robaste?

Apaga mis enojos,
pues que ninguno basta a deshacellos,
y véante mis ojos,
pues eres lumbre dellos,
y sólo para ti quiero tenellos.

Descubre tu presencia,
y máteme tu vista y hermosura:
mira que la dolencia
de amor, que no se cura
sino con la presencia y la figura.

BRIDE

O who can heal my wound!
Quickly, surrender to me now.
  As of today, please send
  me no more messengers
who cannot tell me what I want.

  All those who wander here
inform me of your thousand graces,
  yet each word is a blow,
  and they keep babbling bits
of mystery–leaving me near death.

  And how do you go on,
O life, not living where you live,
  when arrows from the lover,
  which are conceived in you,
fly deep in you–making you die?

  Why do you wound my heart
and then refuse to make it heal?
  And since you took it from me,
  why do you leave it now,
abandoning the thing you robbed?

  Let my sufferings cease
for there is no one who can cure them;
  let my eyes see your face,
  you are their only light;
for you alone I care for them.

  Reveal your presence to me
and kill me by your gaze and beauty.
  See how the suffering
  of love is only cured
when you–or when your face–is near.

¡Oh cristalina fuente,
si en esos tus semblantes plateados,
formases de repente
los ojos deseados,
que tengo en mis entrañas dibujados!

¡Apártalos, amado,
que voy de vuelo!

ESPOSO

        Vuélvete, paloma,
que el ciervo vulnerado
por el otero asoma,
al aire de tu vuelo, y fresco toma.

ESPOSA

Mi amado, las montañas,
los valles solitarios nemorosos,
las ínsulas extrañas,
los ríos sonorosos,
el silbo de los aires amorosos.

La noche sosegada
en par de los levantes de la aurora,
la música callada,
la soledad sonora,
la cena que recrea y enamora.

Cazadnos las reposas,
que está ya florecida nuestra viña,
en tanto que de rosas
hacemos una piña,
y no parezca nadie en la montiña.

Detente, cierzo muerto;
ven, austro, que recuerdas los amores,
aspira por mi huerto,
y corran sus olores,
y pacerá el amado entre las flores.

O crystal brook, if on
the silver surface of the water
you instantly might form
the eyes I most desire!
I feel them in me like a scar!

Look away, my love,
Im going to fly!

BRIDEGROOM
            My dove, turn back,
for now the wounded stag
is climbing up the slope,
freshened by the breeze of your flight.

BRIDE
My love, the mountains and
the solitary wooded valleys,
the unexpected islands,
the loud sonorous rivers,
the whistling of the loving winds.

The night of total calm
before the rising winds of dawn,
the music of a silence,
the sounding solitude,
the supper that renews our love.

Catch us the little foxes,
our vines already are in bloom;
while we take a handful of
the roses for our spray
let no one in the hills appear.

Stop, north wind of death
and come, south wind recalling love.
Breathe on my garden, let
aromas swell the air,
my love will graze among the flowers.

ESPOSA

¡Oh ninfas de Judea,
en tanto que en las flores y rosales
  el ámbar perfumea,
  morá en los arrabales,
y no queráis tocar nuestros umbrales!

  Escóndete, carillo,
y mira con tu haz a las montañas,
  y no quieras decillo;
  mas mira las compañas
de la que va por ínsulas extrañas.

ESPOSO

A las aves ligeras,
leones, ciervos, gamos saltadores,
  montes, valles, riberas,
  aguas, aires, ardores,
y miedos de las noches veladores.

  Por las amenas liras
y canto de serenas os conjuro
  que cesen vuestras iras,
  y no toquéis al muro,
porque la esposa duerma más seguro.

  Entrádose ha la esposa
en el ameno huerto deseado,
  y a su sabor reposa,
  el cuello reclinado
sobre los dulces brazos del amado.

  Debajo del manzano,
allí conmigo fuiste desposada,
  allí te di la mano,
  y fuiste reparada,
donde tu madre fuera violada.

BRIDE

O virgins of Judea,
while the perfume of amber hangs
   on flowers and the rose tree,
   live in some far-off place
and dont appear before our door!

Hide, my darling, and turn
your face to look upon the mountains,
   and dont tell what you know
   but look at friends of her
who goes to legendary islands.

BRIDEGROOM

O birds on easy wings,
lions, stags, leaping fallow deer,
   mountains, valleys, shores,
   waters, winds, passions
and terror in the watchful nights.

With the song of the sirens
and graceful harp, I ask you now
   to put an end to anger
   and not to touch the wall
so that the bride may sleep in peace.

My bride has gone into
the pleasant garden she desired,
   and lies upon the grass
   happy, resting her neck
in the gentle arms of her love.

Under the apple tree
you came and were engaged to me;
   there I gave you my hand
   and you were then redeemed
where once your mother had been raped.

ESPOSA

Nuestro lecho florido,
de cuevas de leones enlazado,
en púrpura tendido,
de paz edificado,
de mil escudos de oro coronado.

A zaga de tu huella
las jóvenes discurren al camino
al toque de centella,
al adobado vino,
emisiones de bálsamo divino.

En la interior bodega
de mi amado bebí, y cuando salía
por toda aquesta vega,
ya cosa no sabía,
y el ganado perdí, que antes seguía.

Allí me dio su pecho,
allí me enseñó ciencia muy sabrosa,
y yo le di de hecho
a mí, sin dejar cosa;
allí le prometí de ser su esposa.

Mi alma se ha empleado,
y todo mi caudal en su servicio:
ya no guardo ganado,
ni ya tengo otro oficio;
que ya sólo en amar es mi ejercicio.

Pues ya si en el ejido,
de hoy más no fuere vista ni hallada,
diréis que me he perdido,
que andando enamorada,
me hice perdidiza, y fui ganda.

BRIDE

Our flowery bed is safely
hidden among the lion caves,
under a purple tent
erected in deep peace
and capped with a thousand gold shields.

Young girls wander about
the roads seeking a sign from you
in the falling lightning
or in the scented wine
which emanates a holy balm.

Deep in the winevault of
my love I drank, and when I came
out on this open meadow
I knew no thing at all,
I lost the flock I used to drive.

He held me to his chest
and taught me a sweet science. In-
stantly I yielded all
I had—keeping nothing—
and promised then to be his bride.

I gave my soul to him
and all the things I owned were his:
I have no flock to tend
nor any other trade
and my one ministry is love.

If Im no longer seen
following sheep about the hills,
say that I am lost, that
wandering in love I let
myself be lost and then was won.

De flores y esmeraldas
en las frescas mañanas escogidas,
haremos las guirnaldas,
en tu amor florecidas,
y en un cabello mío entretejidas.

En sólo aquel cabello,
que en mi cuello volar consideraste,
mirástele en mi cuello,
y en él preso quedaste,
y en uno de mis ojos te llagaste.

Cuando tú me mirabas,
tu gracia en mí tus ojos imprimían:
por eso me adamabas,
y en eso merecían
los míos adorar lo que en ti vían.

No quieras despreciarme,
que si color moreno en mí hallaste,
ya bien puedes mirarme,
después que me miraste,
que gracia y hermosura en mí dejaste.

ESPOSO

La blanca palomica
al arca con el ramo se ha tornado,
y ya la tortolica
al socio deseado
en las riberas verdes ha hallado.

En soledad vivía,
y en soledad ha puesto ya su nido,
y en soledad la guía
a solas su querido,
también en soledad de amor herido.

On cool mornings we shall
find emeralds and flowers, and make
a garland for your hair,
blossoming in your love
and then looped in a lock of mine.

You stared at that one lock
of windblown hair you saw against
my nape, and on my neck
you were a prisoner
gashing yourself in one of my eyes.

When first you looked my way
your eyes printed your grace in me
and made me feel a woman,
and so my eyes could love
all things which they observed in you.

Do not despise me if
you find the color of my flesh
is brown. Look at me well,
and then see how you
endowed me with your grace and beauty.

BRIDEGROOM
The white tiny dove
flew back to the Ark carrying a frond
and now the turtledove
has come upon her mate
on the green borders of the river.

She lived in solitude,
in solitude she made her nest
and all alone her lover
led her in solitude,
wounded in solitude by love.

ESPOSA

Gocémonos, amado,
y vámonos a ver en tu hermosura
al monte o al collado,
do mana el agua pura;
entremos más adentro en la espesura.

Y luego a las subidas
cavernas de la piedra nos iremos,
que están bien escondidas,
y allí nos entraremos,
y el mosto de granadas gustaremos.

Allí me mostrarías
aquello que mi alma pretendía
y luego me darías
allí tú, vida mía,
aquello que me diste el otro día.

El aspirar del aire,
el canto de la dulce filomena,
el soto y su donaire,
en la noche serena
con llama que consume y no da pena.

Que nadie lo miraba,
Aminadab tampoco parecía,
y el cerco sosegaba,
y la caballería
a vista de las aguas descendía.

BRIDE

Let us be happy, darling,
and see us mirrored in your beauty
on mountains and the hills
where limpid waters plash;
let us go deeper in the wood.

And then we'll climb high, high
to peaks riddled with stony caves
safely hidden away,
and there we'll go inside
and taste the pomegranate wine.

There you will reveal
to me the things my soul desired,
and in a flash, O love,
there you will restore
what but a day ago you gave to me.

The breathing of the air,
song of a tender nightingale,
the fresh exquisite grove,
serene and secret night
of flame that burns and gives no pain.

No one was looking there,
no shadow of Aminadab;
the siege was quieted,
and then before the waters
the cavalry descended into view.

ROMANCE 1

Sobre el Evangelio in principio erat Verbum *acerca de la Santísima Trinidad*

1 En el principio moraba
el Verbo, y en Dios vivía,
en quien su Felicidad
infinita poseía.

2 El mismo Verbo Dios era,
que el principio se decía;
él moraba en el principio,
y principio no tenía.

3 El era el mismo principio;
por eso de él carecía;
el Verbo se llama Hijo
que del principio nacía.

4 Hale siempre concebido,
y siempre le concebía,
dale siempre su substancia,
y siempre se la tenía.

5 Y así, la gloria del Hijo
es la que el Padre había,
y toda su gloria el Padre
en el Hijo poseía.

6 Como amado en el amante,
uno en otro residía,
y aquese amor que los une,
en lo mismo convenía.

7   Con el uno y con el otro
en igualdad y valía:
tres personas y un amado
entre todos tres había.

8   Y un amor en todas ellas
y un amante las hacía;
y el amante es el amado
en que cada cual vivía;

9   que el ser los tres poseen,
cada cual lo poseía,
y cada cual de ellos ama
a la que este ser tenía.

10   Este ser es cada una,
y éste sólo las unía
en un inefable nudo
que decir no se sabía.

11   Por lo cual era infinito
el amor que las unía,
porque un solo amor tres tienen,
que su esencia se decía;
que el amor, cuanto más uno,
tanto más amor hacía.

BALLAD 1

In principio erat verbum,
Regarding the Most Holy Trinity

1. In the beginning was the Word, and He lived in God, in whom He possessed infinite happiness. 2. The same Word was God, who was said to be the beginning; He was in the beginning and had no beginning. 3. He was himself the beginning and therefore had no beginning. The Word is called Son, who was born at the beginning. 4. Thus God had always conceived Him and was always conceiving Him and always giving His substance and always possessing it. 5. And so the glory of the Son is what the Father had, and the Father possessed all His glory in the Son. 6. As the lover in the beloved, each one resided in the other, and this love that united them was the same to each one. 7. One and the other were the same in equality; there were three Persons and one beloved among all

the three. 8. And one love in them all made them one Lover; and the Love is the beloved in which each one lived. 9. For the being that the three possess, each one of them possessed, and each one of them loves Him who had this being. 10. This being is each one, and this alone united them in an ineffable knot beyond words. 11. Therefore, the love which united them was infinite, for the three had one Love, which is their essence, and the more love was one, the more love there was.

ROMANCE 2

De la comunicación de las tres Personas

1   En aquel amor inmenso
que de los dos procedía,
palabras de gran regalo,
el Padre al Hijo decía,

2   de tan profundo deleite,
que nadie las entendía;
sólo el Hijo lo gozaba,
que es a quien pertenecía.

3   Pero aquello que se entiende,
de esta manera decía:
Nada me contenta, Hijo,
fuera de tu compañía.

4   Y si algo me contenta,
en ti mismo lo quería;
el que a ti más se parece,
a mí más satisfacía.

5   Y el que nada te semeja,
en mí nada hallaría;
en ti sólo me he agradado
¡oh vida de vida mía!

6   Eres lumbre de mi lumbre,
eres mi sabiduría,
figura de mi substancia,
en quien bien me complacía.

APPENDIX

7   Al que a ti te amare, Hijo,
a mí mismo le daría,
y el amor que yo en ti tengo,
ese mismo en él pondría,
en razón de haber amado
a quien yo tanto quería.

BALLAD 2

On the Communication among the Three Persons

1. In that immense love which proceeded from the two, the Father spoke words of great affection to the Son, 2. of such profound delight that no one understood them; only the Son rejoiced in them, for they belonged to Him. 3. But what He understood He said this way: Nothing contents Me, Son, but your company, 4. and if something pleases Me I love that thing in You. He who resembles You satisfies me most, 5. and he who is nothing like You will find nothing in Me. I am pleased in You alone, Life of my Life! 6. You are the light of My light, you are My wisdom, the image of My substance, in Whom I was very pleased. 7. I will give Myself to him who loves You, My Son, and the love I have in You is the same that I will have for him, because he has loved the One Whom I loved so much.

ROMANCE 3

De la creación

1   Una esposa que te ame,
mi Hijo, darte quería,
que por tu valor merezca
tener nuestra compañía.

2   Y comer pan a una mesa,
del mismo que yo comía;
porque conozca los bienes

que en tal Hijo yo tenía.
Y se congracie conmigo
de tu gracia y lozanía.
3   Mucho lo agradezco, Padre,
el Hijo le respondía,
a la esposa que me dieres,
yo mi claridad daría,
4   para que por ella vea,
cuánto mi Padre valía,
y cómo el ser que poseo,
de su ser le recibía.
5   Reclinarla he yo en mi brazo,
y en tu amor se abrasaría
y con eterno deleite
tu bondad sublimaría.

BALLAD 3

On the Creation

1. My Son, I want to give You a bride who will love You, who
because of her worth deserves to share Your company, 2. and
eat bread at Our table, the same one at which I eat, so that she
might know the good which I have had in such a Son, and that
she might rejoice with Me in Your grace and full beauty. 3. I
am very grateful, Father, the Son answered. I will show My
brightness to the bride you give Me, 4. so that by it she may
see how great My Father is, and how the being I possess I
received from Your being. 5. I will hold her in My arms, and
she will burn in Your love, and with eternal delight she will
exalt Your goodness.

PROSIGUE 4

1   Hágase, pues, dijo el Padre,
que tu amor lo merecía:
y en este dicho que dijo,
el mundo criado había.

2   Palacio para la esposa,
       hecho en gran sabiduría;
       el cual, en dos aposentos,
       alto y bajo, dividía.

3   El bajo de diferencias
       infinitas componía;
       mas el alto hermoseaba
       de admirable pedrería.

4   Porque conozca la esposa
       el esposo que tenía,
       en el alto colocaba
       la angélica jerarquía;

5   pero la natura humana
       en el bajo la ponía,
       por ser en su compostura
       algo de menor valía.

6   Y aunque el ser y los lugares
       de esta suerte los partía,
       pero todos son un cuerpo
       de la esposa que decía.

7   Que el amor de un mismo esposo
       una esposa los hacía:
       los de arriba poseían
       el esposo en alegría;

8   los de abajo en esperanza
       de fe que les infundía,
       diciéndoles que algún tiempo
       él los engrandecería.

9   Y que aquella su bajeza
       él se la levantaría,
       de manera que ninguno
       ya la vituperaría.

10   Porque en todo semejante
       él a ellos se haría,
       y se vendría con ellos,
       y con ellos moraría.

11   Y que Dios sería hombre,
       y que el hombre Dios sería,
       y trataría con ellos,
       comería y bebería.

12   Y que con ellos continuo
      él mismo se quedaría,
      hasta que se consumase
      este siglo que corría,

13   cuando se gozaran juntos
          en eterna melodía;
          porque él era la cabeza
          de la esposa que tenía.

14   A la cual todos los miembros
      de los justos juntaría,
      que son cuerpo de la esposa,
      a la cual él tomaría

15   en sus brazos tiernamente,
          y allí su amor la daría;
          y que así juntos en uno
          al Padre la llevaría.

16   Donde el mismo deleite
      que Dios goza, gozaría;
      que, como el Padre y el Hijo,
      y el que de ellos procedía,

17   el uno vive en el otro;
          así la esposa sería;
          que dentro de Dios absorta,
          vida de Dios viviría.

BALLAD 4

On the Creation (continued)

1. Let it be done, then, the Father said, for Your love has deserved it. And having said these words, He created the world, 2. a palace for the bride made with great wisdom, and divided into two rooms, one above and one below. 3. The lower one was composed of infinite differences but the one above was made beautiful with marvelous jewels, 4. so that the bride might know her Bridegroom. In the higher sphere the order of angels was placed, 5. but human nature was placed in the lower, for man was in his composition a lesser thing. 6. And though beings and places were divided in this way, all are part of one body which is called the bride; 7. for

the love of one bridegroom has made them all one bride. Those above possessed the bridegroom in joy; 8. those below lived with hope based on the faith which He infused in them when he said to them that one day He would raise them up; 9. and He would raise them from their lowness in such a way that no one would insult them any more, 10. for he would make Himself wholly like them, and would come with them and live with them; 11. and God would be man and man would be God, and He would talk with them, and eat and drink with them; 12. and He would remain with them constantly until the consummation of this period of the world, 13. when they would join together in eternal song; because He was the Head of the bride He had, 14. and all the members of the just would be joined in Him; they form the body of the bride, whom He would take 15. tenderly in His arms and there give her His love; and thus when they were joined as one, He would lift her to the Father, 16. where she would rejoice in the same joy which God rejoices in. For as the Father and the Son—and He who proceeds from them— 17. live in one another, so it would be with the bride; for absorbed within God she will live the life of God.

PROSIGUE 5

1   Con esta buena esperanza
       que de arriba les venía,
       el tedio de sus trabajos
       más leve se les hacía;

2   pero la esperanza larga
       y el deseo que crecía
       de gozarse con su esposo,
       continuo les afligía.

3   Por lo cual con oraciones,
       con suspiros y agonía,
       con lágrimas y gemidos
       le rogaban noche y día,

4   que ya se determinase
       a les dar su compañía.

Unos decían: ¡Oh, si fuese
en mi tiempo el alegría!
5   Otros: Acaba, Señor;
al que has de enviar envía.
Otros: Oh si rompieses
esos cielos, y vería
6   con mis ojos, que bajases,
y mi llanto cesaría;
regad, nubes de lo alto,
que la tierra lo pedía,
7   y ábrase ya la tierra,
que espinas nos producía,
y produzca aquella flor
con que ella florecería.
8   Otros decían: ¡Oh dichoso
el que en tal tiempo sería,
que merezca ver a Dios
con los ojos que tenía,
9   y tratarle con sus manos,
y andar en su compañía,
y gozar de los misterios
que entonces ordenaría!

BALLAD 5

On the Creation (continued)

1. Through this good hope which came to them from above, the
tedium of their labors was lightened. 2. But the long waiting
and growing desire to rejoice with their Bridegroom grieved
them continually. 3. Therefore, with prayers, sighs and suf-
fering, with tears and moaning they implored Him night and
day 4. to agree to grant them His company. Some said: If
only this joy would come in my time! 5. Others: Come, Lord,
send the One Whom you are to send! Others: If only the
heavens would break open and with my own eyes 6. I might
see You descending, then my lament would end. Clouds, rain
down from above, for the earth needs you, 7. and let the
earth open wide which has given us thorns, and bring forth
that flower that would be the earth's flowering! 8. Others
said: O what joy for him who would be living in a time when

he might see God with his own eyes, 9. and touch Him with his hands, and walk in His company, and enjoy the mysteries which He will then ordain!

PROSIGUE 6

1   En aquestos y otros ruegos
gran tiempo pasado había;
pero en los postreros años
el fervor mucho crecía.

2   Cuando el viejo Simeón
en deseo se encendía,
rogando a Dios que quisiese
dejalle ver este día.

3   Y así, el Espíritu Santo
al buen viejo respondía
que le daba su palabra
que la muerte no vería

4   hasta que la vida viese,
que de arriba descendía,
y que él en sus mismas manos
al mismo Dios tomaría,
y le tendría en sus brazos,
y consigo abrazaría.

BALLAD 6

On the Creation (continued)

1. In these and other prayers a long time had passed, but in later years a fervor grew intense   2. when the aged Simeon burned with desire, and implored God that he might see this day,   3. and so, the Holy Spirit answered the good old man, giving him His word that he would not see death   4. until he saw the Life descend from the heights, until he took God into his own hands, and holding Him in his arms, pressed Him to himself.

Prosigue la Encarnación

1   Ya que el tiempo era llegado
en que hacerse convenía
el rescate de la esposa
que en duro yugo servía,

2   debajo de aquella ley
que Moisés dado le había,
el Padre con amor tierno
de esta manera decía:

3   Ya ves, Hijo, que a tu esposa
a tu imagen hecho había;
y en lo que a ti se parece
contigo bien convenía;

4   pero difiere en la carne,
que en tu simple ser no había;
en los amores perfectos
esta ley se requería,

5   que se haga semejante
el amante a quien quería,
que la mayor semejanza
más deleite contenía.

6   El cual sin duda en tu esposa
grandemente crecería
si te viese semejante
en la carne que tenía.

7   Mi voluntad es la tuya
(el Hijo le respondía)
y la gloria que yo tengo
es tu voluntad ser mía.

8   Y a mí me conviene, Padre,
lo que tu Alteza decía,
porque por esta manera
tu bondad más se vería.

9   Veráse tu gran potencia,
justicia y sabiduría;
irélo a decir al mundo
y noticia le daría
de tu belleza y dulzura
y de tu soberanía.

         APPENDIX

10   Iré a buscar a mi esposa,
       y sobre mí tomaría
       sus fatigas y trabajos
       en que tanto padecía.

11   Y porque ella vida tenga
       yo por ella moriría,
       y sacándola del lago
       a ti te la volvería.

BALLAD 7

The Incarnation

1. Now that the time had come when it would be good to ransom the bride, who was serving under a hard yoke, 2. under that law which Moses had given her, the Father spoke tenderly, in this manner: 3. Now You see, Son, that Your bride was made in Your image, and insofar as she is like You she suits You very well; 4. yet she is different in her flesh, which Your simple being did not have. In perfect love this law was in effect: 5. that the lover become like the one he loves, that the greater their similarity the greater their delight. 6. Surely Your bride's delight would greatly increase if she were to see You like her, in her own flesh. 7. My will is Yours, the Son replied, and My glory is that Your will be Mine, 8. and what Your Highness said is agreeable to Me, because in this way Your goodness will be more clearly seen. 9. Your great power will be seen and Your justice and wisdom; and I will go and tell the world, spreading the word of Your beauty and sweetness and of Your dominion. 10. I shall look for My bride and take upon Myself her weariness and labors from which she suffers so much. 11. And that she may have life, I shall die for her, and lifting her out of the deep, I shall return her to You.

ROMANCE 8

Prosigue

1   Entonces llamó a un arcángel,
que San Gabriel se decía,
y enviólo a una doncella
que se llamaba María,

2   de cuyo consentimiento
el misterio se hacía;
en la cual la Trinidad
de carne al Verbo vestía.

3   Y aunque tres hacen la obra,
en el uno se hacía;
y quedó el Verbo encarnado
en el vientre de María.

4   Y el que tenía sólo Padre,
ya también Madre tenía,
aunque no como cualquiera
que de varón concebía;

5   que de las entrañas de ella
él su carne recibía;
por lo cual Hijo de Dios
y del hombre se decía.

BALLAD 8

The Incarnation (continued)

1. Then he called an Archangel, known as Gabriel, and sent
him to a virgin known as Mary,   2. at whose consent the
mystery took place, in whom the Trinity clothed the Word
with flesh.   3. And although three performed the deed, it was
done through the one; and the Word lived incarnate in Mary's
womb.   4. And He Who had only a Father now had a Mother
too, but she was not like others who are conceived by man.   5.
From her own flesh He received His flesh, so He is called the
Son of God and of man.

ROMANCE 9

Del nacimiento

1   Ya que era llegado el tiempo
en que de nacer había,
así como desposado
de su tálamo salía,
2   abrazado con su esposa,
que en sus brazos la traía,
al cual la graciosa Madre
en un pesebre ponía,
3   entre unos animales
que a la sazón allí había:
los hombres decían cantares,
los ángeles melodía,
4   festejando el desposorio
que entre tales dos había;
pero Dios en el pesebre
allí lloraba y gemía,
5   que eran joyas que la esposa
al desposorio traía;
y la Madre estaba en pasmo
de que tal trueque veía:
6   el llanto del hombre en Dios,
y en el hombre la alegría,
lo cual del uno y del otro
tan ajeno ser solía.

BALLAD 9

The Birth

1. Now that the time had come for Him to be born, he went
forth like the bridegroom from His bridal chamber, 2. em-
bracing His bride, holding her in His arms, He whom the
gracious Mother had borne in a manger 3. among animals
which were there at that time. Man sang songs, angels melodies,
4. celebrating the marriage which was taking place between
these two. But God wept and moaned there in the manger,
5. tears which were jewels that the bride brought to the
wedding, and the Mother gazed in wonder at such an ex-
change: 6. in God was man's lament and in man was joy,
which things were usually so alien to each one of them. Finis.

PRINCIPAL VARIANT TITLES
AND SUBTITLES

1   *a.* Noche oscura
    b. Canciones del alma que se goza de haber llegado al estado de la perfección, que es la unión con Dios por el camino de la negación espiritual
    c. Canciones del alma
    d. Canciones en que canta el alma la dichosa ventura en pasar por la *oscura noche de la fe,* en desnudez y purgación suya, a la unión del Amado

2   *a.* Cántico espiritual
    b. Canciones entre el alma y el esposo

3   *a.* ¡Oh Llama de amor viva!
    b. Canciones del alma en la íntima comunicación de unión de amor de Dios
    c. Canciones que hace el alma en la íntima unión con Dios

4   *a.* Entréme donde no supe
    b. Coplas del mismo sobre un éxtasis de alta (harta) contemplación

5   *a.* Vivo sin vivir en mí
    b. Coplas del alma que pena por ver a Dios

6   *a.* Tras de un amoroso lance
    b. Otras del mismo a lo divino

7   *a.* El pastorcico
    b. Otras canciones a lo divino de Cristo y el alma

8   *a.* La fonte
    b. Cantar del alma que se huelga de conocer a Dios por fe

9   *a.* Super flumina Babylonis
    b. Romance que va por *Super flumina Babylonis*

SELECTED BIBLIOGRAPHY

EDITIONS

Anzoátegui, Ignacio B. *Obras escogidas: San Juan de la Cruz.*
5th ed. Madrid: Espasa-Calpe, 1964.
Blecua, José. *Poesías completas y otras páginas.* Zaragoza: Ebro,
1946.
Crisógono de Jesús, Matías del Niño Jesús, Lucinio del Ss.
Sacramento. *Vida y obras de San Juan de la Cruz.* 4th ed.
Madrid: Biblioteca de Autores Cristianos, 1960.
Salinas, Pedro. *Poesías completas, versos comentados, avisos y
sentencias, cartas.* Madrid: Tauro, 1936.
Silver de Santa Teresa, P. *Obras de San Juan de la Cruz.* 5
vols. Burgos, 1929-31.

TRANSLATIONS

Campbell, Roy. *The Poems of St. John of the Cross.* Preface
by M.C. D'Arcy, S.J. London, New York: Pantheon Books,
1951.
Nims, John Frederick. *The Poems of St. John of the Cross.*
New York: Grove Press, 1959.

STUDIES

Alonso, Dámaso. *La poesía de San Juan de la Cruz.* 3rd ed.
Madrid: Aguilar, 1958.
Baruzi, Jean. *St-Jean de la Croix et le problème de l'expérience*

mystique. Bibliothèque de philosophie contemporaine. Paris: Félix Alcan, 1924.

Brenan, Gerald. "Studies in Genius–II: St. John of the Cross, His Life and Poetry." *Horizon,* May 1947: 256–81; June 1947: 324–56.

Father Bruno. *St. John of the Cross.* London, New York: Sheed and Ward, 1958.

Father Crisógono de Jesús. *The Life of St. John of the Cross.* London: Longmans; New York: Harper and Row, 1958.

Guillén, Jorge. "The Ineffable Language of Mysticism: San Juan de la Cruz." *Language and Poetry.* Cambridge, Mass.: Harvard University Press, 1961.

Milner, Max. *Poésie et vie mystique chez Saint Jean de la Croix.* Paris: Aux Editions du Seuil, 1951.

Orozco Díaz, E. *Poesía y mística: introducción a la lírica de San Juan de la Cruz.* Madrid: 1959.

Peers, E. Allison. *Spirit of Flame: A Study of Saint John of the Cross.* London: SCM Press, 1961.

Sobrino, J.A., S.J. *Estudios sobre San Juan de la Cruz y nuevos textos de su obra.* Madrid: Consejo Superior de Investigaciones Científicas, 1950.

———. *La soledad mística y existencialista de San Juan de la Cruz.* Madrid: 1952.

Spitzer, Leo. "A Method of Interpreting Literature: *En una noche oscura." Smith College Lectures.* Northampton, Mass., 1949, pp. 21–45.

Complete descriptive catalog available free on request from
New Directions, 333 Sixth Avenue, New York 10014.   † Bilingual